POST-
LOUGH
1945–1

C000150335

HOW WE WERE AND
HOW LOUGHTON
CHANGED

BY

TERRY CARTER

EDITED AND WITH AN INTRODUCTION BY

CHRIS POND

LOUGHTON
LOUGHTON AND DISTRICT HISTORICAL SOCIETY
2006

First published in 2006 by
Loughton and District Historical Society
and available from Forest Villa, Staples Road
Loughton, Essex
IG10 1HP

Reprinted 2010

www.loughtonhistoricalsociety.org.uk

Front Cover: The Crown, Summer 1963

Designed and typeset in Linotype Palatino by
Ted Martin

Cover design and repro by
Artform
Little Tew
Oxon OX7 4JH

Printed in Great Britain by
Sudbury Print Group
Sudbury
Suffolk

Contents

Illustrations

The Crown, Summer 1963: *front cover*
Plate 1. Loughton Carnival Week 1951 – Festival of Britain Carnival float prize list. The judges include a famous operetta star, an artist, architect, the town clerk and three councillors: *inside front cover*
Frontispiece: Council Offices decorated for Queen Elizabeth's Coronation, June 1953. On the back it says: 'Decorations hired, erected and removed by Jas Smith & Co Ltd. In position from from May 30th–June 22nd @ £38': *page 6*

Between pages 64 and 65:
Plate 2. Loughton High Road in the 1930s – almost identical in 1945 but the Gas Light & Coke Co's showroom was built on the vacant plot – later Café Rouge
Plate 3. The High Road – London Cooperative Society supermarket (almost the UK's largest at the time) – October 1965
Plate 4. The High Road, 29 June 1969 – probably still the best preserved section
Plate 5. The Gardeners' Arms, April 1965 – cottages adjacent are about 400 years old
Plate 6. Smarts Lane weatherboarded cottages – still unchanged in 1969 – number 45 is second from right
Plate 7. An almost empty Smarts Lane in 1958 – and the British School (boys)
Plate 8. The British School now – a private house – March 2006
Plate 9. Off to Southend or Clacton – author is front row, 7th from right
Plate 10: Forest Road, May 1945 – off to celebrate VE Day! The children include: Brian Hornsby (next to wheel), Kenny Boyling (far right), Trevor Marcussen (at rear), Ken Moore (by lamp), Brian Austin (bomber jacket), Daphne Mitchell (white ribbon), Sheila Moore (top), June Law (over wheel). The horse is Jack Street's and Mr Austin senior is the adult. The ladies with the pram are thought to be from Smarts Lane. Photo courtesy of Lily Austin
Plate 11. Loughton Cinema, 1928 – later the Century – closed in 1963 with only 40 of its 600 seats occupied on its last night.
Plate 12. Former site of Loughton/Century Cinema – April 1968
Plate 13. The Crown, circa 1960. Patmore Bros's Garage behind
Plate 14. How the view has changed – March 2006
Plate 15. Staples Road Schools – drawn by Robert Barltrop and reproduced by permission of the *Newham Recorder*. This is the former Girls', and Infant, School of 1911
Plate 16. Staples Road School – dear Miss Jenkins' class of 1949
Plate 17. Eaton Brothers' Fordson lorry *LVX 781*, in Meadow Road, 1949, my father (Dick) driving
Plate 18.Victor's Handyman's Shop – 1968
Plate 19.Victor's old site in March 2006
Plate 20. Willow Cottage, Loughton High Road, during demolition – March 1967
Plate 21. The Willows, March 2006
Plate 22. The Holly Bush, 8 February, 1970 – the alley to Smarts Lane has long been closed
Plate 23. Newnham House 1962 – making way for an extensive development of flats
Plate 24. The Broadway, Debden – 28 March 1965
Plate 25. Loughton War Memorial and the King's Head (now Zizzi) – 29 April 1970

4

Introduction

When I wrote the introduction to Gertrude Green's autobiography in 2004, I made the point that Loughton now possessed an almost complete library of reminiscences dating back some 125 years, but that this stopped short at about 1950. I was very pleased when, a few weeks later, Terry Carter contacted me and said he was willing to fill the gap.

Personal memories are very important to local history. In the early 20th century, local historians were mostly concerned with piecing together the religious, tenurial and genealogical records of their communities. They often did this with great assiduity and scholarship, but perforce they could illustrate very little of what life was actually like in their parishes in the past.

There are those who would say that personal memories are trivial, subjective, and a less serious contribution to local history than archival studies. With this, I profoundly disagree. True, memory can be fallible and selective, but when combined with reference to documentary sources, it is a most valuable instrument to local history, and it can illustrate the realities of life in the past which a more learned and academically based study cannot.

For that reason I have been particularly pleased to have edited Terry Carter's narrative, which is such a full account of post-war Loughton. Where else have we an account of the privations of rationing and the practical steps Loughtonians took to remedy them? The Festival of Britain, aspects of the town's two carnivals, and the attitudes to the newcomers to the Debden LCC Estate are thoroughly rehearsed here.

Terry Carter says that this narrative is in some ways a repayment of the debt he owes Loughton, but I think Loughton is in fact in Terry's debt, for chronicling, so faithfully and in such detail, its history in our times.

CHRIS POND
May 2006

Frontispiece: Council Offices decorated for Queen Elizabeth's Coronation, June 1953. On the back it says: 'Decorations hired, erected and removed by Jas Smith & Co Ltd. In position from from May 30th–June 22nd @ £38': *page 6*

Preface

When Gertrude Green's excellent book *My Life in Loughton* was published at the end of 2004, my wife bought a copy, which we both read with particular interest. It was reviewed in the local *Guardian*, under the headline 'One historical society in search of an author'. We found Mrs Green's memories fascinating but, apart from a few later recollections, they end well before the 1950s, so the Loughton and District Historical Society were seeking somebody to, as it was reported, 'complete the story'.

Mrs Green lived at 69 Smarts Lane. I was in No 73, but we were exact next-door neighbours, as there was no 71. Anyway, it seemed appropriate to offer myself to have a try.

Many of those who have penned their memories of Loughton were either born, or lived for a long time in Smarts Lane or Forest Road, by common consent the poorest roads in the old town. As mentioned, I am no exception, spending my first 23 years, from April 1941 to our marriage in March 1965, in 'The Lane', although in the course of the following pages I will try to include recollections and impressions of many other parts of the town.

By coincidence, at the time of embarking on these reminiscences, almost the last 23 years have also been spent here, although in a different road. As well as the total of nearly 46 years in Loughton itself, the rest of my time, apart from three years near Chelmsford and several years living in Japan, has mainly been in Woodford and Buckhurst Hill so, as a long-standing local resident, I welcomed the chance given by the Loughton and District Historical Society, to make a little repayment.

Although this small volume deals mainly with the 1950s and 60s, I have gone back a little further, to the latter half of the 1940s. That is where my recollections really begin and, to set the scene for the emergent prosperity of the later decades, it seems logical to include the difficult earlier background, before Loughton's recovery from the War really gathered momentum.

This book is not intended to be a critical comparison of Loughton past and present, and I hope readers will agree with my conclusion that both times have plusses and minuses and that as well as a justification for nostalgia there is also a recognition that times change and that we have to move with them. Neither is it an indulgent attempt simply to write an autobiography, but many memories and some comments are obviously subjective and personal. I have tried to make Loughton itself the reason for undertaking the exercise, to fill the gap highlighted by the Historical Society.

My thanks to Chris Pond for his invaluable editorial skills and assistance and to Ted Martin for his patient adaptation of my output into the proper format. There are also a few others who have provided information: they wish to remain nameless, but they know who they are.

TERRY CARTER
May 2006

1 Overview

Before thinking about Loughton in the 1950s and 60s, you really need to reflect a little on life in the town in the years immediately following the Second World War. As I was born in 1941, it is fortuitous that the first real memories I have begin from the age of four or five, conveniently leading into the main period covered by this book.

In those early years Loughton was my little world, one I left very seldom, and life as it affected me and those of my age was simple. At the time we had little inkling of the social and structural changes that were already under way here, but looking back, the aftermath of War was very tough, especially for those in the poorer streets.

We all know that the whole world was still hung over from the Second World War, with slow recovery, and widespread deprivation and that English life was austere and we all hated ration books, shortages, 'export only', Black Markets, utility clothes and furniture. However, Loughton, especially when compared to many northern parts of England, undoubtedly recovered faster than the average, probably helped by being so close to London and the City. I have tried to provide some recollections of the changes in those post-war years and their effect on different parts of the town.

As a tonic and a sign of better things, in May 1951 the Labour Government sanctioned the Festival of Britain, although the Government changed in October that year. I went with my parents, and so, I remember, did many of our neighbours and my friends from Staples Road School. We children were totally enraptured; probably the adults were too.

The Dome of Discovery and the Skylon inspired us to aim for and build a new era of prosperity and invention. By 1951 Loughton was also on the way up again. Later I will describe a few signs in our house that, in material terms at least, testified to a tentative ending of self-denial.

Loughton's weather was always better then. But then it always is, looking back. Maybe it's because we spent so much time out of doors in those days, but I'm pretty sure the sun seemed to shine all summer, not only in 1951, but for years before and after, and we had quality snow, not on 1947's overwhelming scale but always enough to sledge down the precipitous Drummaids, the great slope behind the Forest crest opposite Staples Road School, or behind the Warren Wood on the Epping New Road. Small things but forever treasured. I haven't checked any climate statistics, but I don't think this is simply a case of self-delusion, or looking back through a rosy mist.

From the darker side, I remember the personal tragedies and triumphs of families and neighbours from the tough streets and those who were perhaps more privileged, but who still no doubt had hard struggles of their own. I recall the intense pressure to pass the dreaded 'Scholarship', that infernal 11-plus, a huge watershed in those times, sadly a set-in-stone measure of success or failure, and the inevitable destitution I would bring upon myself if I failed.

Epping Forest played a big part in the daily lives of many residents, particularly from those roads, including Smarts Lane and Forest Road, that led straight into it or, like Staples Road, which fronted it directly. In those early post-war years of deprivation, the Forest was a source, albeit unauthorised, of food and fuel, of recreation, an extended school playground, and much, much more. I will try to outline why, years later in the period, it changed, and was less used by Loughton residents, particularly from the Lane and nearby, probably as we could afford motorised transport, and our pleasures became more sophisticated.

I will naturally try to pass on many memories of family life and of the people in the roads I knew best. My street, Smarts Lane, was, for the most part, a close community, and grief and happiness were often shared. Nobody there had a car, so you walked everywhere, played outside and knew everybody. There was much self-help. Once outgrown, clothes were passed on to other families' children. There was no shame in borrowing five bob until the end of the week. I remember passing old comics and books to other families, sometimes eggs from the chickens we kept in the back garden or vegetables from my father's allotment in Roding Road. It was the normal thing to do, and they accepted these things without embarrassment, repaying with favours and errands when they could.

Thinking of the changes in Loughton life, were there winners and losers, or did everybody end up better off? 'Let us be frank about it, most of our people have never had it so good.' True or false, or just 1957 electioneering, Harold Macmillan, for this part of West Essex?

When the period started, Loughton probably still had a clearer social defining line than most. Did we all worship in the same places? 'Rich man in his castle, poor man at his gate?' The War, a great social leveller, may have heralded the end of those days, but some vestiges lingered. So how did residents from the poorer parts interact with the more affluent? Did the 50s and 60s accelerate the ending of 'service' in the town?

Did Loughton have to make adjustments when the new LCC Debden Estate was built? Or when the pre-fabs came, or the River Estate?

What happened in Loughton if you were ill? Or your teeth hurt? What about the 'nit-nurse' and the school dentist?

Who were the calling tradesmen and where did they go? What happened to all the little shops? How did we move from buying little and often from specialist traders to the celebrity opening of one of the UK's earliest supermarkets and one-stop shopping?

Friends, enemies, relatives, school, sport, shops, medical services, church or Sunday School, the Forest, architectural disasters, shameful town planning and demolition, all these and more leave tiny digital imprints about Loughton in the brain. Although many are gone, some can be recaptured and brought to its forefront as vivid memories.

There are others, of course, of later times, also poignant and colourful, but looking back, the 50s and 60s do seem very special years, with many previously closed doors now open. I hope to show that, for the most part, it was an uplifting period for our town.

2 Origins

Before embarking on my memories of Loughton in the 1950s and 1960s, of some of the people, and how our lives and the town changed, a mixed bag of the good and the bad, I have to go back to the beginning. Although my recollections are sharpest from about 1950 onwards, some scene-setting from the 40s is relevant.

As mentioned in the preface, I am a *bona fide* Loughton native, born in 1941 in a tiny end of terrace cottage, 45 Smarts Lane. Strangely, thanks to Chris Johnson in his very helpful *Loughton Street Names – a History*, I learned that our road once featured as 'Carter's Lane' in 1790 before the present name was first used in 1819, in reference to a Matthew Smart, a resident of the time. A 'Carter's Cottage' – 63 Staples Road – was built about 1900.

I was the only child. My mother, Anne Lottie Carter was from Cheshire Street, Bethnal Green, one of three sisters. There was also a half-sister. My father Richard, always Dick, was a Loughton man from No 45, the younger of two brothers.

Harry, the elder brother, but called 'Young Harry' to differentiate him from 'Old Harry', his father, lived next door in 47, in the middle of the terrace of three, with his wife May, and Ron, my cousin, also an only child. 49, the third and last of the terrace, (which was not shown on the 1929 records, so presumably was added later) was home to Bert, my grandfather's brother, his wife Freda and Leslie, their daughter. Like many properties in and around the Lane, all three were probably rented from Chiswells, who I also remember later as having an antique and reproduction furniture business in York Hill and, later, in Forest Road.

Apart from the eleven Carters in 45 to 49, there were another five in 131 Smarts Lane: George, his wife, two sons, Jeff and Gordon and a daughter, Greta, my second cousins. There were a few others in the Lane and Forest Road, but they were unrelated.

My mother had served an apprenticeship with Selfridges as a top class dress machinist, working for them for 10 years or so before being given the chance to join the buying department, where she stayed until she married my father. He worked for a Covent Garden firm, driving lorries and vans, delivering fruit and vegetables until early in the Second World War when he joined the Royal Engineers. Young Harry went into the Navy.

My parents met in the West End while my father was on leave and on a later break from service in 1940 they married in Epping Registry Office.

So No 45 was shared for a few years with Mary and Old Harry, that is, my Nan and Granddad. He was originally a Waltham Abbey man, whose first job was working in the munitions factory, and on the barges carrying deadly explosives around the country. Later, when he moved to Loughton, he would often walk the whole way to the factory and back. He eventually left to work for Foster's, the biggest Loughton builders of the time, whose premises were conveniently exactly opposite his house. Nan was from Poplar. Neither had much formal education and, in truth were barely literate but, like many in the Lane, they were certainly street-wise. They had been married in St Mary's in the High Road, and she always said how different it was at the time of their wedding. I can't recall exactly what she meant by that, except that, around 1910, the church still had open fields at the back.

I'm told there were tensions in those early days, partly because of the crowded conditions, worries about the brothers away in the War, also because of the uneasy mix of a faster-paced East Ender landing in a parochial, semi-rural new family. Maybe there were testing times, but these apparently eased off later, as everybody was in the same boat, mucking in, getting on with life as best they could.

3 Earliest years and the move to No 73

Houses in the Lane were, even in the forties, already old: some I believe, maybe 90 years or more. Most of the properties were rented, some, as mentioned, from Chiswell's, others from Gould's, another prominent firm, who also owned the granary on one of the High Road's largest frontages. In 1941, when I was born, 45 Smarts Lane was a Chiswells property but there is a 1929 record of it being rented to my grandfather by George Perry, a prominent local resident. From when I was old enough to compare, to well into the 50s, I knew nobody in Smarts Lane, or in Forest Road, who had a bathroom or inside lavatory. Although there have been so many accounts of life in 'two up, two down' cottages, with sculleries and a big stone copper, the old cast-iron grate in the minuscule back room, galvanised baths hanging by the back door, outside lavatories with newspaper squares hanging from the nail in the wall, the old mangle and washboard, gas lighting, I will still add my own.

There were indeed two small gas-lit living rooms downstairs in No 45, inevitably called the 'back' room, where day-to-day life was spent, and the 'front' room, almost a waste of valuable space, so little was it used – nothing unusual in that, it was normal for Smarts Lanites and Forest Roaders to keep it for best. Upstairs, as you would expect, there were two tiny bedrooms of identical dimensions to the rooms below, with no facilities, except a big water jug and bowl in each, plus the 'gazunder', the good old chamber pot, and a good supply of candles and the safer stubby nightlights in metal holders.

Gas, coal gas, smelly and dangerous, was on a forties' version of 'pay as you go' with the sealed meter under the stairs, kept going with shillings stored in a jar on the mantelpiece. It was quite usual for neighbours who forgot to top up their jars or tins to knock for a 'shilling for the gas'.

Like many in the Lane, 45's scullery was long and low-ceilinged, with a butler sink, a copper and a gas stove and with plenty of room to drag the bath in for the ritual Friday night soak. It was a slog to fill it with endless bowls and kettles of hot water either heated on the gas cooker or lifted from the copper itself. Getting the temperature right was an art, and one of the few things I remember clearly about those years is having kettles poured into one end of the bath while I huddled down the other then, on stretching, leaping out in panic to escape a scalding as the hot water reached my backside.

The copper was really a concrete urn, kept whitewashed, with a thick wooden lid and a grate underneath for the coals which, once burning away, were closed off by a cast-iron door with a slider to open and close the air vents. It did the job though, and also did brilliantly in the making of steamed puddings and anything else that was lowered into it. Pease-pudding was a particular gem. Some years later, like many of our neighbours' stone coppers, it was demolished to make way for a gas one, mottled blue, I remember, and just like a big, glorified tea urn.

Many, if not most of Smarts Lane and Forest Road houses that I knew had the 'grate', a kitchen range in the back room. Most winter days and nights would be spent crowded round this gleaming cast-iron focal point, kept safely back by the big brass fender around it. All the neighbours I can remember had one, some shining more than others, with the oven on one side, heated by the hot coals. Serving as fire, stove, oven, grill and toaster, it was amazingly versatile. We had ours in No 73 for many years after leaving 45, and I remember dangling thick slices of bread in front of it on a charcoal-stained three foot long wire fork. I believe many ranges were supplied by Nicholls and Clarke, in Shoreditch, under the brand name 'Niclar'.

The 'back bricks', as Nan called them, of 45, 47 and 49 were a concrete area about 15 feet by 10, outside the scullery door, religiously washed down every week, summer and winter. Each of the three was divided from its neighbour by a tall creosoted, slatted fence, which then ran the full length of each garden. However, each fence had a door cut into it, halfway down the bricks, and all three families moved freely through these from one cottage to the next. This arrangement was fairly common in Loughton (for example in Staples Road) and was not only done because families were related. The front doors of 45 to 49 stayed unlocked, often even at night, long after this early period, well into the 60s, but there was never any feeling of insecurity.

It wasn't just us: many houses in the Lane and Forest Road were the same all the years I lived there, that is, to 1965, and no doubt beyond. From spring through to autumn, on fine days many front doors would stay open, and the residents would often pull a kitchen chair into the doorway, or onto their gleaming front step and either watch the world go by, reading the paper, probably the *Daily Mirror*, sometimes knitting or sewing to supplement their small incomes, perhaps simply 'to make do and mend' while enjoying a pleasant neighbourly gossip.

Unsurprisingly, I don't remember too much about the Lane in my first three or four years, certainly not of the town itself. I must have been wheeled or toddled 'round the village' countless times but nothing really comes back to me.

Most of my memories of No 45 are from the times I mention later, after we left there, as hardly a day went past in the next dozen or so years without a call on Nan or May and Harry next door.

It was sometime late in 1944, when my father was on leave, that he heard from the landlord that a larger house in Smarts Lane had become available. Army pay wasn't a lot, but he had some savings, more of which later, so, able to afford the rent, they took the chance and moved up the road to No 73. According to *Kelly's Directory of Loughton* in 1939, 73's tenant was a Mrs Purkis, and I assume it was she who, for whatever reason, vacated the house. In 1929 Frederick Purkis, presumably her husband, was the tenant, and a Miss Addis the owner of 73 and 75. Miss Addis also owned 42 Forest Road, which in 1929 was the building contractors, Warriner and Herd's (related to but not the same as Warriner the funeral director) shop/yard that now after various incarnations, houses a high quality wood flooring business. 73 Smarts Lane backs directly onto those premises.

Our neighbour in No 75 was Miss Alice Reynolds, who I remember well, and liked very much. She was listed as the tenant in 1929, and may well have been there earlier still. Over the years I would happily run errands for her, and I mean no disrespect to her memory in pointing out her diminutive size. She was indeed a lady of very restricted growth, probably not even four feet tall. On the other side, in No 69, as mentioned in the preface, was Mrs Gertrude Green, of *My Life in Loughton* fame.

There was no number 71. Why not? I had thought that what probably happened was that, when the semi-detached houses occupied by Miss Reynolds and my family were originally built, in the early 1900s, they were much larger than the older terraced cottages on the site and on either side. Possibly another terrace, comprising 75, 73 and 71, was demolished and three houses replaced by just two but, to avoid any re-numbering of the houses, 71 simply became history, and was never used again. However, there is another possibility to explain the absence of 71. Chris Pond points out that Smarts Lane was numbered in 1904, around the time 75 and 73 were built, and that the Loughton UDC probably allowed for three to be erected, although only two were actually constructed. We both remember a plaster mould under the eaves showing a date, possibly 1907, but this, unfortunately, is now only a blank circle.

So we moved in 1944. I have very limited recall of that year and the next but there are a few things I remember clearly. No 73, like 69 and many others, had an Anderson shelter, dug into the end of the garden. Years later, my father relocated it and turned it into a coal and wood shed. I have no recollection of ever going into the Anderson, but I can remember sleeping in the Morrison shelter, the flat steel and wire construction that was in our front room, also serving as a table. It was in that that I heard the drone of aircraft that passed over the town, some of which had it seems, veered away from London to avoid lethal anti-aircraft fire. My 10-year-old cousin, Maureen, now a local resident, but then a beleaguered East-ender, who sometimes came to stay with us in Loughton, would say either 'Don't worry, it's one of ours' or perhaps, more worrying, as German planes had a distinctive rumble to them, 'That's a Heinkel'.

One night a German thrumming was followed by several huge explosions, much too near, which we heard and felt. We found out the next day that a stick of bombs, incendiaries I think, had been jettisoned in Epping Forest, inside and outside the boundary of Fairheads' Nursery in Nursery Road.

Ron, my cousin, retrieved most of the case of what he and the neighbours called a Molotov Breadbasket. I remember it. It was silver and had sharp, curved fins at the end. Collecting shrapnel was a favourite occupation of many kids, not just from Loughton, so this was a highly prized object. It was rather beautiful, in a sinister sort of way, even though the business part was gone. Why Molotov, I don't know, although I seem to remember later talk of lots of these having being dropped on Russia.

It was that stick that left the three craters I remember, 10 or 12 feet across and maybe 2 feet deep, on the Stubbles, the big clearing off Nursery Road. They were parallel to Fairhead's boundary, and would, in wet weather, fill up to make small ponds. In later years, playing cowboys and Indians, or soldiers, I can remember lying flat in them, hidden from view of the prowling enemy. There was a much bigger dip on the other side of the Stubbles, created in the same way, I was told. It was a lot deeper, and always full of water and it even, I don't know how, came to contain a variety of fish. It was surrounded by prolific blackberry bushes, a wonderful source of supply for jam-makers in the Lane and Forest Road, probably other roads, too.

The Stubbles craters/ponds were finally deemed to be a safety hazard and filled in sometime around the mid-50s, and I remember that, for some reason, the blackberry bushes were also cleared at the same time.

Happily, that time nobody was hurt. Many bombs and much shrapnel fell harmlessly into the Forest but, sadly, there were fatal bombings in the district, and in Loughton itself. These, such as the one in Habgood Road, have been well documented before, but I don't remember them myself. Gertrude Green refers to the tragic death of William Clarke, hit by 'friendly' fire from one of our own anti-aircraft guns. He is among the civilians now commemorated by a plaque erected on the front of Loughton police station. Over the years my mother and his widow, Win, became close friends, and I played club cricket with her son, Douglas, now deceased, a very accomplished all-rounder, for over 10 years from 1956. Harry and Dick came back unscathed from the Second World War, but counting the names on the War Memorial in front of what I will always call the King's Head, irrespective of the name on it now, 64 men from Loughton gave their lives in that awful conflict.

Some husbands, including some from the Lane and Forest Road, through a variety of reasons, including illness, died or vanished and even though neighbours helped out, it was very tough for some.

Ironically, the only casualty in our family was me. My father, home on leave from Europe, was showing me how his Lee-Enfield rifle worked and, pulling back the bolt, accidentally fired it while my finger was in the empty breech. It was a bad cut, but was only bandaged, never stitched, so to this day I can display the jagged scar on my right forefinger and claim it as a genuine war wound.

4 Beyond the family circle

The overwhelming feeling in the Lane was that the ending of the war in Europe had to be celebrated properly, and that meant we, like thousands of other streets, enjoyed a big VE day party, draping Union Jacks from front room windows, stretching bunting across the road the whole length of the street, and joining tables loaded with mostly home-made food in a long line outside Grimsleys, the butchers. Somebody produced a gramophone and a load of dance music. That, and a general exuberant sing-song to patriotic Vera Lynn records, kept everybody going until late, but then, in the morning, it was back to thinking about getting themselves, the Lane, and Loughton going again, in fact, simply to start over, to try making a reasonable living.

Loughton had to get restarted properly, as the town, and the village High Road in particular, was a big source of employment, largely in the shops and service providers. Also, although rapid social changes were seen as the years went by, at that time the Lane and Forest Road also provided many of the town's daily helps, ladies that 'did' for those in wealthier roads.

Luckily, when the two brothers, Dick and Young Harry came home from the War and were then demobbed, they immediately had jobs to go to. My father applied to join Eaton Brothers, builders, of 47–49 Meadow Road, the firm where he stayed until retiring in the late 70s. He started as a driver/handyman, but added many strings to his bow, including roofing, his later speciality. Most roofs in Smarts Lane, Forest Road, and many in other parts, including the High Road and Church Hill, were of dark grey slate, and I always thought a new slate roof rather grand.

Young Harry joined Foster's, directly opposite No 45, where Old Harry was also employed, later switching to Essex Steel Scaffolding, which shared the same yard. They both kept their navy blue demob suits for many years, until thickening waistlines forced them to be sent to the jumble sale.

Local builders, vital employers, had plenty of work in the years after the War, not just run of the mill decorating, repointing or roofing, but also, with government subsidies, putting right a great deal of war damage. Eatons, Fosters, and Diggens, among others, undertook such repair work not only in the district, but also further out, right into London. I can remember in the 1949 or 1950 summer holidays, being taken in my father's lorry, a Fordson, LVX 781, a number I have never forgotten, as he delivered bricks, cement, sand and scaffolding to sites in East London and the City. I clearly recall parking near London Bridge, then climbing the Monument together for breathtaking views of the capital still being slowly mended.

Many houses in Loughton's poorer roads were gradually being brought a little more up-to-date, building restrictions permitting, with improvised indoor sanitation and, in a few cases, mainly beginning with residents with better paid jobs, a proper bathroom, but invariably on the ground floor, not upstairs.

It was not until 1953 that we took that final step, and at last, after years of fiddling around, adding on bits and pieces, managed a full upgrade of No 73. Some readers, used to modern sophistication, may not fully appreciate just how uplifting that was but, believe me, it was wonderful. That downstairs bathroom lasted 48 years, until my mother died in 2001. It was strange perhaps, that when the house was sold a year later, the buyers were the building firm that now occupy Eaton Bros' former premises, where my father worked for almost 35 years, over half his life. Chris Pond has told me that towards the end of 2005 planning permission was given to demolish 47–49 Meadow Road, and to build two houses. That made me even more aware of the relentlessness of changes in the town.

Our household was luckier than most, we were able to move ahead a little and, like other kids, I began to be more aware of the world outside the front door. Taken literally, stepping beyond the family circle and into the street was no problem in 1945, as there were few cars, certainly not in the Lane or Forest Road. Houses with garages were mostly in well-to-do roads such as Connaught Avenue, Connaught Hill, Ollards Grove, Spring Grove, others too, even more grand, like Tycehurst Hill, Spareleaze Hill, and the poshest of them all, Alderton Hill. It was in these that Loughton's Austins, Morrises or Fords, and sometimes much more prestigious makes, had been kept mothballed while the War was on, preserving precious fuel, only emerging again some time after it was over, having been taken off the bricks or wooden blocks sometimes used to raise them up to stop their tyres from perishing. So the streets were safe, even for four and five-year-olds although, to make certain, the old look right, look left, look right again mantra was well and truly drummed into us from that early age.

In September 1945, not yet five, I took my first big step outside, probably the biggest of all, one of the main rites of passage, starting school which, for most of my age, meant Staples Road Infants, a pivotal and integral part of the lives of children in the town whose parents either could not afford to pay for private education, or had the confidence to rely on Staples Road anyway.

From the thrill of that very first day in the Infants, until leaving the Juniors in July 1952, I loved the place and, looking back, feel that nowhere else could have been better, despite the dodgy plumbing in the freezing outside lavatory blocks and the sometimes intemperate throwing of chalk or blackboard dusters by certain male teachers. True, some pupils fared less well, and perhaps one or two I recall, who were deemed to be backward children, but who later did reasonably well, were possibly dyslexic, a condition not acknowledged in those days. One boy that I particularly remember was always put out of the way at the back of the class, which surely only made learning even harder for him.

Those first school years were fundamental in shaping the direction of our lives and I believe we in Loughton were as well served as you could expect anywhere. Staples Road, and the other schools I remember, either as a pupil or through other contact, will naturally crop up frequently in these reminiscences.

5 A mixed recovery

Recovery after the Second World War was obviously toughest for the Loughtonians mentioned earlier, whose husbands or other close family members had been killed or wounded but, even setting such tragic cases aside, progress in the town's general standard of living seemed mixed. Loughton was certainly much better off by the time the 50s ended, and a large number of us perhaps agreed with Macmillan that 'most of us have never had it so good'. Many residents, particularly my generation of friends, felt a confidence that carried on through the 60s, but getting to that point had not been easy at first. For varying reasons, post-war Loughton life proved much harder for some than others.

We were all affected, until the early 50s, by rationing and shortages that meant putting up with monotonous daily menus, unless tempted by Black Market spivs to buy something that had 'fallen off the back of a lorry'. However, residents in wealthier streets began, in other ways, to recover faster from the War than those in poorer ones. Even though Loughton's favourable location, so close to London, must have been an advantage compared to many other places, my older cousins, Maureen and Ron, remember feeling rather let-down at first, a sense of anti-climax, considering the country's high hopes of better times ahead. A minor example, perhaps, is of the kids in our road thinking they would have as many sweets as they liked but, of course, they ended up disappointed.

In some ways poorer parts of Loughton fared relatively better than wealthier neighbourhoods. The main example was the new NHS and the emerging welfare state. Obviously major blessings to be shared by all, they were clearly worth a lot more to lower income Loughtonian households. A blow for some of the eager young people around the town, particularly from families where an early extra wage would have been most welcome, was that the school leaving age was going up from 14 to 15.

Despite the new benefits – free teeth and glasses, no doctors' bills – and the partial safety net of those early days of social security, some of my neighbours still had to live in very stressful circumstances. A few houses near us were in a really shocking state, cold and damp, with wet rot and dreadful plumbing but, despite repeated complaints to some landlords about these conditions and the high rents, in many cases little would be done to improve the situation. One terraced house only a few doors away from No 45 became virtually uninhabitable and needed to be completely dried out, then to have the downstairs floorboards, including the joists, entirely replaced, and some others in the road were almost as bad. Faced with heavy pressure and the risk of much expense, we heard that certain landlords were thinking to offload some of their properties in the Lane, a fact which immediately interested my father.

In the worst instances of hardship, when the mother would be raising the family on her own, neighbours would help them out. Earlier I listed some items that we, among others, passed on, but as well as clothes, books and home-grown produce, there were even a few occasions with families in particular difficulty, when my father even helped pay their rent, and it was partly his anger over this that indirectly led to our later purchase of No 73 and a big change in our lives.

Except in their tiny living rooms, most houses in the older roads were cold, literally icy sometimes, and winter visits to the often unlit outside lavatory were no joke. When we moved to 73, although there were gas fittings in every room, we did have electricity as well, unlike 45, which stayed completely on gas for several years longer, I remember running errands for Nan and Grandad round to Barton's or Goodrich's in the High Road, Loughton's leading hardware shops, for a fresh box of six mantles, as well as paraffin for the heater they sometimes used upstairs as they got older. They would also heat up house bricks in the oven, wrap them in blankets, and use them instead of hot water bottles. Despite being offered various chances to change to electricity they always declined, saying it was too much upheaval, and that they knew where they were with gas.

Although electricity was available in Smarts Lane from about 1930, few landlords had felt impelled to wire up the cottages. No 47 had only been converted to electricity soon after the War and Uncle Harry had become increasingly frustrated by the old folks' refusal to follow suit, so he decided to take drastic action to prove its advantages. He bought a long cable and ran it through 47's back room window frame, along the outside wall, through the slatted fence, in through a hole drilled into 45's window, before screwing a hook into the living room wall which then supported a bulb socket and switch. This Heath Robinson device worked extremely well, so finally, into the 50s, electric light lit up one solitary room in the old cottage, and Nan and Granddad had at least, although not exactly with Electricity Board approval, partly caught up with the times. Soon after, every room in the house was wired up properly.

Loughton, for many reasons, remains a great place to live, but I have very fond memories of the post-war town as almost rural compared to now, calmer and more relaxed. Sometimes, looking at old 40s and 50s photos of the town centre, I am still amazed that Loughton was so unhurried in those days, but it really was. However, inevitable change was in the offing. Today, if you look at older roads off the High Road such as Smarts Lane, Forest Road, Meadow Road and to a lesser extent, High Beech Road, which was a rung or two higher up the social ladder, you see evidence of changes that began in the more optimistic 50s and accelerated through the prosperous 60s, then beyond. In the first two roads there was a rather satisfying mixture of long rows of cottages, mostly brick, although a number were of white or black weatherboard, a few modest shops, pubs, various builders' yards and other assorted business premises. The appearance of some parts has, even now, stayed much the same but others, particularly in the 60s and 70s, were sometimes altered almost beyond recognition.

For example, demolishing the lovely spired building, which many readers will no doubt remember as Victor's, a handyman's shop, but formerly an old bakery, on the site of what is now the cramped little car park on the corner of High Beech Road and Smarts Lane, instantly converted a pleasant semi-rural view into a shapeless mess. There had been rumours and protests for a year or so before the bulldozers finally moved in around 1970. Another section of this book deals with some of the much earlier 60s architectural misfortunes that befell Loughton, the High Road especially, in the name of progress.

In the early to mid-60s, with double glazing then becoming popular, some residents in the old houses, desperate to shut out persistent cold and draughts, sometimes opted for lower quality units or mismatching porches. There were many conspicuous mistakes, but those were probably an understandable price to pay for modern comforts, certainly better than suffering frost on the inside of your windows or having to plug whistling gaps with felt or rolls of plastic foam.

Houses in the wealthier roads, where improved, were rather more sympathetically extended and altered, or vacant plots filled in with similar properties to those already built. Those streets generally appeared much the same through the 50s and 60s, and it always struck me as strange how middle class Loughton roads, where professional and business workers and their families lived, always seemed so tidily quiet. Loughtonians who owned cars garaged them, or at the very least stood them on their driveways and, because the two-car family was so rare in those days, there was hardly any parking in the road. There were probably as many children living in those roads as in ours but whenever I walked along them they must either have been indoors or out for the day, as so few youngsters seemed to be playing outside. Perhaps they played in the commodious gardens, read more books, even watched more television.

With cars on the road again, despite the petrol rationing that lasted to the beginning of the 50s, some of us used to be quite envious when our better off Staples Road classmates described their drives to the seaside. With beaches no longer forbidden territory, seaside resorts were open for business again and some children would be taken there for a week, even a fortnight, in the summer holidays, something almost unknown in Smarts Lane. However, many less well-off families tried to compensate in other ways and quite a number of our neighbours would regularly take the family to Southend, a bus and train journey of nearly 2½ hours. For four or five years, until I left Staples Road, our summer Sunday routine, if the weather looked reasonable, would be the same – up at the crack of dawn, make the sandwiches, catch the 167 bus from the Crown to Ilford Station, then take the steam train to Southend Victoria for the long walk down the hill to the beach – on weekdays you could catch a 2/6 illuminations special. Saturday trips weren't possible as my father, like many neighbours, always had to work a 5½-day week. Like most men in the building trade, he was paid by the hour, and had to fill in weekly time sheets, so time off hit them straight in the pocket.

Occasionally Smarts Lane and Forest Road would combine to hire a charabanc, even two sometimes, for a trip, also normally to Southend. These popular bookings were often made through Charlton's, the High Road newsagent close to the former Loughton Cinema, renamed the Century. We would board in the Carpenters' Arms car park, or outside the Victoria Tavern, then enjoy the ride, before parking behind the old Kursaal, the permanent fairground nicely convenient for the beach. We would often be back late, with some of the men sometimes rather the worse for wear after an extended stop at the Halfway House, a big pub on the Southend Road. A real favourite but, for some reason, not with me, was a coach to see the Southend lights, which in the early 50s was undoubtedly the most dazzling spectacle within our reach.

Early in that period it was mainly lower-paid workers who rented small places like ours and, to boost the family income, many of the wives had to clean houses in wealthier streets. We paid rent for 73 for nearly seven years until 1951, and my father always complained it was money better kept in the bank, rather than in a landlord's pocket. For most of that time, because the living conditions of some less fortunate families mentioned earlier had so irritated him, he was saving hard to buy the house. At the same time, now I was at school, my mother did what many of our neighbours had to do, and began cleaning houses in wealthier parts of the town. In those days married women with young children hardly ever worked full-time, as many schoolchildren, including Staples Road pupils, went home for lunch. Many husbands who worked locally, including Dick, also often returned home around midday, so going back to dressmaking in the West End wasn't an option for her.

Part-time jobs in shops were hard to find but, even though the pay was poor, there was still a big demand in Loughton for domestic helps. Her first cleaning job was in Spring Grove, for the Erridges, a job she saw advertised in a newsagent's window, and she worked there for about 10 years. That family had a love of dachshunds, and, after a while, we often looked after them when they went on holiday – Mitzi first, then after she died, Fritzi – both were much loved by us. She also cleaned other houses in Church-fields, for the Palfreys – Mr Palfrey was Deputy Clerk to Chigwell UDC – The Drive, The Avenue and, briefly Sedley Rise, near the old Loughton bus garage, As she walked to all these places, the Sedley Rise job meant the long climb up Church Hill to the north end of town so she soon gave that one up. Those roads may have been much less grand than some where the houses were really superior but, outside and inside, they still impressed me greatly, and it was partly through occasional visits to those places I first began to realise that, much as I appreciated the Lane, there was something else to aim for.

Because I often visited both Eatons' yards in Meadow Road, I became friendly with some of the families there, particularly two or three with children at Staples Road. This cul-de-sac is another old road, consisting of small brick cottages with slate roofs built well before 1900, although there were several bigger double fronted places, and some housewives there were also cleaning larger houses.

I don't remember many real complaints about others being better off than us, but my mother would sometimes talk about the ways in which 50s daily life was easier in houses where she worked. Washing machines, Hoovers and refrigerators were becoming everyday items for many middle class Loughton homes, but she, like most of the neighbours, was still doing her daily chores the hard way, with brooms and brushes, the old mangle outside, a wooden clothes horse squeezed in front of the grate and even, as we used ourselves in No 73, old black irons heated on the gas stove, her hands protected by quilted squares made by my Nan from scraps of material. Nan, and many of the elderly ladies around us used to make great numbers of those colourful iron or pot holders for local bazaars and garden fêtes.

In those days, although there were definitely haves and have-nots in Loughton, if you were the latter you simply got on with things. I would have to say yes if asked whether there was still class consciousness in post-war Loughton, but our neighbours accepted it as a fact of life, and one that might be changing anyway. In the early days of the Debden Estate snobbish views were expressed, particularly by older residents, about new people being different. There were also occasional smug comments at school about classmates from below, i.e. east, of the railway line, based, I suppose, on either simple geography or, more likely, the fact that many of those families were also relative newcomers to the town.

An interesting comment made by Caroline Pond is that at this time there were also some residents that could be described as 'in-betweens', i.e. such as those from the Habgood and Roding estates who were owner-occupiers rather than mainly renters, the latter being the norm in Smarts Lane and Forest Road.

I only came across real deep-seated class resentment when I worked in the Holly Bush, more of which elsewhere. There were a few young men who always used the public bar, one of whom had a degree in Russian from London University, who were so passionate about redistribution of wealth that George Smith, the publican in the 50s and 60s, often had to step in and shut them up, or else they would be asked to leave.

Strange things happened on and just before Boat Race day and, what-ever your social standing in Loughton, it simply ceased to matter. Only relatively few Loughtonians went to any university in the early 50s, let alone managing to enter Oxford or Cambridge, and yet the Boat Race was followed with a great passion all over town. For some years, probably as far as the early 50s, there would be street vendors outside Woolworths offering light or dark blue favours, such as rosettes, flimsy windmills and cheap tin badges and, under our breath, we school kids would ask each other 'Are you Oxford or Cambridge?' as if it meant faithful friend or mortal enemy. Whether from Smarts Lane, Roding Road, Ollards Grove or Woodbury Hill, this was an exciting event shared equally by all classes and roads, and yet at that time many rowers in the two boats probably repre-sented the very apex of privilege.

My parents were all but teetotal before they married, but almost as soon as Dick came back from the War, to help the savings along they completely gave up both smoking and their very modest drinking. He mended our shoes, doing it very professionally, with leather and rubber from Pryke's, the shoe-menders in Forest Road, using a proper metal last, and also grew most of our fruit and vegetables in the back garden or on his allotment.

Although their main objective was to buy No 73, in order to offset the general feeling of late 40s austerity, in about 1948 my parents indulged us in a major luxury. They lashed out on a new Bush radio, a polished walnut giant powered from the mains, so we no longer had to use cumbersome accumulators or the slab-like blue Ever Ready or red Vidor batteries. It was still working perfectly in 2001, over 50 years later, when my mother died.

A couple of years later we bought our first television, a Ferguson, from Escott Bros, a popular electrical shop in the High Road, at the crossroads with The Drive and Brooklyn Avenue. Its monstrous cabinet housed a ridiculously tiny 9-inch screen, and the instructions that came with the set were crazy. It was recommended that for every inch of screen width you should sit one foot away, not very practical in a room only ten feet wide, so we soon abandoned that idea and huddled much closer. The old 40s and 50s programmes certainly enthralled us then, no matter how antiquated the occasional grainy black and white clips may seem now.

There were relatively few televisions about until the 1953 Coronation created quite a TV boom, so a regular group of seven or eight Smarts Lane kids came to our house and avidly watched the children's programmes, particularly the serials. A real favourite was the long-running *Mystery Squadron*, and we would howl in frustration if the dreaded card came up, 'Normal service will be resumed as soon as possible'. The late Allan Eaton, a member of the building family, and no doubt remembered by many present Loughton residents as a very well respected local electrician, kept that old Ferguson going for years.

In 1950 there could have been a major setback to my father's plans. Completely out of the blue, Mr and Mrs Reginald Evans acquired 73 and the house next door, 75, having moved in there after Miss Reynolds, the tiny lady, died. After they became our new landlords my father thought the Evans's would continue to use 73 as an investment but, over a year later, having realised he was serious about buying the house, they offered it to him for £500, a considerable sum in 1951 and by no means a bargain price considering its age. Dick tried unsuccessfully to negotiate a better deal, but in the end he had no real option but to accept.

As Reg Evans himself told me some years later, the Evans had no idea how hard my parents had been saving, and were sure Dick would have a lot of trouble raising the money, so perhaps the most triumphant moment of my parents' lives was when they went round the village to Attwater & Liell, then, as now, leading Loughton solicitors, who were acting for both sides, to complete the purchase. Having been to the Midland Bank in the morning, in the afternoon they handed the solicitor a large brown envelope containing the full purchase money. They had taken over six years to scrape it together.

It was probably about 25 years or so later that those workmen's cottages became much sought after as starter homes, chic bijou residences, as enthusiastic estate agents called them, and really started to fetch amazing prices. However, even by the late 60s, with many of the little cottages extended and modernised, the poorer parts of Loughton were starting to be considered up-and-coming parts of town. A good friend of mine, the late Tony Swallow, lived in Smarts Lane in the 50s and 60s. He will be remembered by many current Loughtonians for the efforts he made on behalf of the town for several years through his services as a local councillor and in 1967, his year of office as Chairman of the Chigwell UDC.

6 Loughtonians and Epping Forest

Fruits of the Forest

Whichever decade you look at, if you think about Loughton you naturally reflect on Epping Forest, whose 6,000 acres are one of the last remnants of the vast woodland once covering much of East Anglia. Many have described its beauty, the commercial advantage it added to the town and the turbulent times when its very survival was at stake.

Some 30% or so of the land area of Loughton *is* Epping Forest; and yet, despite all that it offers, I know most people from the town nowadays rarely set foot in it. That is unlikely to change, as many Loughton residents hardly seem to walk anywhere much now, but hop into the car to supermarkets, load up, and drive home. Driving along forest roads, they may well appreciate the scenery, but putting on Wellingtons or trainers and having a wander around seems very low on their wish list. Whenever I walk through it, mainly with my granddaughter on her bike, it seems a pity that other humans are so scarce.

It wasn't like that when my parents regularly took me into the forest when my father came back from the War, after which we, and many other Loughtonians, took frequent advantage of it and were thankful for all that it offered. Partly with the help of POWs, it had been cleared of shrapnel and other war debris, including high explosives. Then, just as now, it was magnificent, although maybe some parts were more overgrown, while plains such as the Stubbles and Fairmead Bottom were, unlike now, mainly clear of trees and shrubs.

I think there was a more basic difference that faded as we entered the optimistic 50s and prosperous 60s. This distinction was that because of shortages in the 40s and early into the next decade the forest, as well as being a scenic attraction, was an actively used source of food and fuel. For some Loughtonians, Epping Forest meant they could supplement meagre food rations and tight budgets, as well as providing an excellent reason to get out and about in those times when few had television and there was limited transport other than shanks' pony or a bike. Schools used it for sport and lessons – Staples Road certainly did, more than most of course, as it was literally on the doorstep.

Although it helped fill understocked Loughton larders in ways that may have been unauthorised, many residents, especially from the poorer part of the town, accepted that as entirely justified. For several years after returning to civvy street, my father and the two Harrys certainly took advantage of the fact that, less than five minutes from the house, they were in the forest, and 10 minutes later could be setting up to catch a rabbit for the pot. They, like others I knew, kept ferrets and nets and their way of thinking was simple – why keep a ferret or a polecat unless you intended to use it?

Their usual hunting ground was behind the Gravels, or Strawberry Hill Pond, as it is shown on forest maps. Behind the Gravels and down to the Epping New Road were numerous rabbit warrens, maybe not as large as some at the end of Nursery Road near The Warren itself, on which City of London management of the forest is based, or those bordering the nearby Fairmead Bottom – the Bottoms, as we called it. Rabbits were probably more abundant in those places, but it was more risky to catch them.

Their technique needed to be different to the organised methods of much earlier times, when barking dogs would be used to scare feeding rabbits into lines or enclosures of nets. Young Harry would take his spaniel, Pat, and Dick had our fox terrier/Jack Russell cross, Floss, with him, normally before first light on Sunday, prior to the rabbits coming out to graze. With the dogs made to stay completely silent, one of the brothers would set the green nets at the exits of the warren. The ferrets would be slipped into the entrance tunnels to flush out the rabbits, which would then rush headlong into the nets for a quick dispatch. The dogs would guard unnetted holes, and force the rabbits back if they tried to escape.

The system worked well, they normally came home with six or so between them and, as far as I remember, they never lost a ferret. They let many rabbits go as they only set out to catch what was needed, not to be greedy, nor to make any profit, and would regularly give some to neighbours who were either elderly or hard up.

When they came home, the rabbits would be taken from their overcoat pockets, and Harry, who had been a butcher in the past, would skin and clean them out. Harry and Dick loved animals, and they never used snares or other traps that caused suffering. They, especially Old Harry, also knew the forest keepers well, and he was mostly on friendly terms with them. It has been suggested in places that relations between the forest keepers and Loughton residents were often hostile. Perhaps, but that was never the experience in our family nor, as far as I am aware, among our neighbours. Yes, Old Harry always said those men knew exactly what was going on but in all the years he and his sons went after rabbits, or simply walked in the forest, they were never troubled by the keepers, nor treated with anything but respect.

As the rationing situation improved rabbiting gradually declined, but what finally ended it completely was the onset in the early 50s of the awful affliction, myxomatosis, the virus which swept through and almost eliminated the rabbit population, more so in Epping Forest than many other woodlands. I remember the first time I encountered the disease, and it is still one of my most distressing memories of the forest.

I was helping Terry and Bobby Howes, who lived in High Beech Road and whose father, Bert, owned a popular greengrocer near the Holly Bush pub, to deliver goods to the big houses in Nursery Road. We had finished, and the big flat handcart we had been using was empty, so we were happily riding it down the slope in Nursery Road, near the junction with Upper Park. There, in the middle of the road, in broad daylight, was a near-dead rabbit, and we then saw several others in distress in the nearby ditch. I won't describe their appalling symptoms but, once seen, never forgotten.

Many Loughtonians used to go wooding, that is gathering up fallen branches, only legitimate provided they did not exceed specified limits – there was an exact allowed size but, as a guideline, anybody stopped by the forest keepers would have to leave gathered wood behind if it was longer than from the neck to the end of a man's arm, stretched sideways, or thicker than a forearm. Helping branches down with a metal bar or a piece of wood on the end of a rope was strictly frowned upon; damaging trees in that way seemed to be viewed more seriously than catching rabbits. The two Harrys and my father had more sense than to antagonise the keepers over a few branches, so they never took liberties and besides, there was always a plentiful supply of discarded timber from Eatons' or Fosters' building jobs, splintered scrap with no other use than for fuel.

There weren't many lawns in the tiny front gardens of Smarts Lane or Forest Road, but several houses were set well back from the road, with plots that were partly grassed over. If their grass became worn, a few of the residents would cut turf from the forest and patch it into their own. That was also not allowed but, although such new turf stood out very clearly, I don't recall any trouble over it.

Removing leaf mould was also illegal, but many Loughtonians would fetch the odd bucketful without a problem. One neighbour though, went too far, and was wheeling a whole barrow load down the Lane when a local policeman spotted him. They knew each other well, but the bobby couldn't simply ignore such a pile of rich compost so, to end the matter, he made him take it back. That neighbour had an allotment in Roding Road, a few strips away from my father's, and he wanted the leaf mould to fertilise it.

I knew several residents who would gather whole baskets of bluebells but my father would never allow it. It seemed so much better to leave them on view in their natural surroundings, along with other wild flowers, especially as bluebells almost instantly go weak and droopy when picked.

However, plenty of fruits and nuts were well worth harvesting. Every October I still go to the Gravels where, bearing half left, there is a sizeable chestnut wood. It is amazing how many nuts are now left to rot, whereas in the 50s and 60s you had to be up very early if you wanted to gather any at all. If the fall had been accelerated by a windy night you had to be about even earlier.

Blackberries, mushrooms, sloes, crab-apples, medlars, rose-hips, chestnuts, beech nuts, acorns, conkers – the menu on offer was a long one, and every one of these was gathered. Of these, conkers were the only item of no

27

real use other than for the children to skewer, string and swing in conker fights. Mushrooms, choice ones, were widespread and it was legal to gather them but, as years passed, and the eating-out habit expanded, many restaurateurs in the 60s began stripping the Forest of them. Nothing was done until several years ago, when it was finally made illegal to pick mushrooms other than under licence, restricted to 1½ kilos a year.

Even ground-up acorns were turned into pancakes by one or two neighbours but, looking back, that seemed a bit desperate, as the result was horrible, as the bitter taste of the tannin, even after endless leaching, still lingered. It was better, as some did, to rake them up for sale as pig food.

Although the 50s and 60s range of wild forest crops remains similar to the present, plentiful shops and forest bye-laws now make much of the list either irrelevant or illegal.

Problems with horses

After the War, horse riding picked up again and the majority of riders then, just as now, enjoyed their pastime properly. However, because my friends and I walked or cycled in the forest so much we saw many instances of some riders behaving not just badly, but sometimes dangerously.

For as long as I remember the Forest has suffered from damage by horses. The paths were particularly affected in the 50s and 60s. Most attempts to limit the abuse, whether through general appeals or notices posted on forest paths, have been largely ignored by successive hard cores of riders. I suppose that young lads in the Lane and Forest Road were more aware of badly ridden horses than many. This was because about 20 of us, mainly from the two roads, but with a few imports from Roding Road and Valley Hill, would assemble on the Stubbles for the Sunday football matches that, from about 1949 to 1954, became a regular feature. Goalposts were coats and teams were either sorted by picking up sides, with the toss of a coin deciding first pick, or very often it was simply Smarts Lane versus Forest Road – for the record, Forest Road won more times than we did.

We were on perfectly good terms with many horse riders, and would normally have no trouble, but there was one particular group that would gallop recklessly from near The Warren, along the forest path, the Green Ride, that still exists, finally pulling up at the Earls Path Pond or, as we called it, the Robin Hood Pond, on the road to the pub of that name. They would sometimes even turn left at the Gravels and run their horses straight into the water, which was never very deep, churning up the mud and silt, regardless of who might be enjoying themselves there, or picnicking, as many did on the raised clearing behind. Protests were useless.

The leader of this group was a very stout man who always dressed in a dark brown jacket and waistcoat plus jodhpurs and a brown hat – what I would now call an Indiana Jones trilby. He would ride full gallop, always on his own at first, up and down one side of the Stubbles, then the other, after which the others would do the same. Whatever made them decide they had to start riding dangerously through the middle, back and forth, I don't know, but they did, laughing, forcing us aside and ruining our matches. Some parents even objected at the police station but nothing came of it.

I won't forget one wet Sunday, the last time we were ever interrupted in that way. They were at it yet again, so Micky Allway, one of the bigger lads, normally very good-natured, shouted at the man in brown, sparking off instant horse rage. Shouting furiously, he dismounted and rushed towards Mick, wielding his riding crop, and lunged at him. All Mick did was step aside smartly, and there was no contact, but the man slipped in the wet, overbalanced and fell flat. Of course, Mick and the rest of us all burst out laughing, but what really upset him was that his cronies laughed too. He tried to remount, but couldn't make it, he was so puffed, so he led his horse into the trees and vanished. That was a minor victory, but some horse riders remained a problem, a bad one at times, for decades afterwards.

When Sandra and I were married in 1965, we moved to Boreham, near Chelmsford, but I always kept in touch with what was happening in Loughton and, as it was something I felt strongly about, I knew that the horse-rider problem was getting worse. A few years later discussions finally took place, no doubt well-intentioned, aimed at limiting the continual damage but nothing much seemed to improve and the problems persisted into successive decades. It will be interesting to see how effective the introduction of licensed riding proves to be. On that question, a friend of mine, a serious amateur naturalist and occasional lecturer on both the Epping and Hainault forests, regrets to tell me that there is, even after the 2003 licensing, a current minority of riders just as uncaring as the ones we encountered on the Stubbles over 50 years ago.

There was a much lighter side. Horses always welcome were the ones sometimes led or ridden up or down Smarts Lane, usually to or from the stables at the bottom of Connaught Avenue. These, plus the coalman's and the rag and bone man's working horses and Robin, who pulled Jack Street's milk cart around Loughton, and was stabled in the dairy only four doors from our house, were prolific providers of much-prized manure, so there were always handy buckets and spades to collect it. Robin did his stuff almost to the end of the 60s when Mr Street retired, ending a family association with Smarts Lane of over 50 years. Rose growers in the Lane sadly missed Robin when our milk was delivered from an electric float.

In the 40s and early 50s many still used the forest for days out, particularly around High Beach, but it was nothing like the heyday of the Retreats, particularly the huge ones like those owned by the Riggs family, which used to swallow up thousands in a day. Inspired by the 19th century expansion of the railways from London into Essex, canny entrepreneurs opened many retreats, serving food and drink, but no beer, to hordes of day-trippers flocking to the forest. My mother-in-law, who is still alive, was one of those, and she clearly remembers being brought to High Beach and Theydon Bois as a small child, on Bank Holiday outings organised by her Methodist Church Sunday School in Tottenham.

Much fascinating information about the retreats is available elsewhere, but they are relevant here in pointing out how visits to Epping Forest declined over the years. In the late 19th century to the end of the 1930s, visitors were prolific; after WWII and into the 50s, numbers fell away greatly but I remember the forest as still very lively; from the 60s to now, it has, by comparison, been a trickle.

The only retreat surviving intact is Butler's Retreat, the small one on the Rangers Road, which is now a fully licensed restaurant, but remnants remain of others much bigger, including the YHA hostel in Wellington Hill and also at High Beach, the home of Fred Speakman, the well-known naturalist. Shaftesbury, the western end of Staples Road, built around 1970, takes its name from the old retreat located there. The Retreat House is still there, unaltered, but the feeding barns were demolished for the houses. For details of this, see the LDHS publication, *From Mean Streets to Epping Forest*, and the interpretation board on site.

After the War, the retreats may have disappeared, but there were still travelling fairs, much bigger than the ones today, on Chingford Plain and, for a time in the late 40s and early 50s, on the old LNER sports ground behind Loughton Station, now the Hanbury Park estate. Also tempting were the mini-fairs, with swing-boats, sometimes a helter-skelter or a small roundabout, toffee apples and roll-a-penny. One continued for a few years at High Beach, but the one nearest to us that I remember was on what was then a much more open green at the top of Forest Road, at the crossroads of Earls Path, Smarts Lane and Staples Road. Mrs Audrey Wood, a Forest Road resident, reminded me that this entertainment was set up by Mr Harrington, and that there were also donkeys and a coconut shy.

That green was on our way to Staples Road School, and is close to Loughton Brook, running from Staples Road Pond, the Reservoir (or the Reservoy, as Old Harry and my Nan pronounced it), into the town. Many times, to or from school, we would go brook jumping there, or to look for frogs and newts, which were plentiful among the water weeds and stones. In the 50s brook jumping was a popular pastime in many other parts of the forest, particularly near Drummaids and around Baldwins Hill Pond. That great pond, as it looked in the late 40s and 50s, will always be my most memorable spot in the whole of Epping Forest.

A regular dare among my classmates and other pupils, which to decline meant a forfeit, was to cross Loughton Brook at Staples Road on the wrong side of the railings, a distance of only a few yards, but with a long drop underneath, using the narrow ledge behind the Reservoir sluice, and without holding on. Also, as at that time the tunnel taking the brook away from there had, unlike now, no protective grille, we used to walk through it for quite a distance. Unquestionably daft, but nobody came to grief. That corner green also used to have an adjacent area under the trees that, in those days, was clear, and it was there a few of us including, I remember, Trevor Marcussen, Frank Curtis, Richard Bathard from Forest Road, all aged about eight, first played cricket, on a leaf mould pitch, with a tree trunk for stumps, and the ball often ending up in the brook.

At weekends many family groups strolled through the forest carrying shopping baskets containing their picnics, and my mother's Bethnal Green relatives would often come over on the steam train or, after 1948, the Tube. Sometimes they took the bus – of which more later. On Sundays there was a special service that continued on to High Beach. It started at Clapham Common and ran for some years and sometimes if we felt lazy we would pick it up at the Robin Hood for the final mile to the Kings Oak, the watering hole for almost two decades of the many fans who went to the nationally famous speedway track that finally closed in the mid-40s. That pub is also remembered by me as being next to High Beach Swimming Pool, that closed about 50 years ago, surely the coldest that ever existed, where we Staples Road pupils had compulsory swimming lessons. These were always early in the morning, rain or shine, and to make it worse we had to walk there and back.

Our family often walked to Lippitts Hill, which had been a POW camp but which was later used in the 60s as a police training centre. We would stop at the old Owl pub, watching sheepish first-timers fall for the old 'beware of the water 'otter' trick, the kettle on the end of a chain dangling in a scruffy galvanised tank full of murky water. When harvest time was over, we would wander back through the cornfields behind the Owl, gleaning broken seed heads and leftover grain on the way, free feed for our chickens.

Smarts Lane and Forest Road children, boys and girls, would play unsupervised but safe on and around the Stubbles and Fairmead Bottom. It was football, cricket, cowboys and Indians for the boys, while the girls would skip or use sticks to mark out floor plans on leaf mould, gravel or clay, and play house. There were always others about enjoying the forest, so even though we were far out of sight of our homes, safety was never a problem, apart from the normal skinned knees and elbows.

If we weren't playing football or cricket a group of boys of mixed ages would sometimes do what we called the Chingford Lake Run. The lake's proper name, Connaught Waters, was not how it was generally known in the Lane. Dick, the two Harrys and other neighbours always called it Chingford Lake. The run began halfway up Smarts Lane, at the Carpenters' Arms, then left across the green at the top of the Lane, along Nursery Road, climbing past The Warren, over the Epping New Road and down to Connaught Waters. We would meander back to the Carpenters for a pint of lime squash, popular with us because it was cheap, poured by Tony Martin or his mother at the tiny off-licence booth at the side of the pub.

Strangely, and to digress, when on a trip to Tokyo in 2001, I was asked by a Japanese lady, who works for a friend there, and who found out I was from Loughton, which she had visited, if I remembered the big lake at Chingford (not, of course actually in Chingford, but shared between Loughton and Waltham Abbey) whose proper name she had forgotten. She had studied in England for a year in 1976, and lived the whole time in Chingford.

We became expert in making quite sophisticated bows and arrows, always from straight holly branches, stripped, polished, with string wound around the middle for the grip. The ends would be notched then strung, ready for the arrows, also cut from the holly. Polished arrows would be slit, and chicken feathers slotted in to make very efficient flights. Those bows could shoot arrows a great distance, but nobody played the fool, and I don't remember any mishaps. A variation on the normal bows and arrows that we used to make was the throwing arrow, which I have never seen anywhere else. This was a longer arrow, thicker too, with a notch cut into the flighted end into which a loose loop of string would be slipped. The string was then tightened and held in the hand as we gripped the sharp end. It might sound complicated but, by throwing the arrow like a cricket ball, and flicking the wrist, the jerk of the string would add amazing distance to the throw, and the older lads could make those things fly almost the length of our Stubbles football pitch.

In about 1953 I learned the folly of smoking. One Sunday morning I was leaning against a tree in the small copse on the Stubbles, clutching an illicit packet of Woodbines. Not wishing to be caught with the evidence, I needed to finish them before going home so, slightly green and groggy, I was madly puffing two at a time. I felt even worse when a back-hander from my grandfather, who crept up behind me, stung my ear. He snaffled the rest, but at least the old boy kept mum about it.

Grey squirrels, even though they wiped out the reds, are always welcome in our garden, but they can be destructive and, I think it was in the mid to late 50s, they were causing far too much forest tree damage. I remember notices nailed to trees offering a shilling for every squirrel killed. I believe you had to take the tails to the forest keepers to collect your money. As I recall, this endeavour flopped and the 1s. offer was withdrawn. I remember being glad.

In the 50s and 60s, as now, commoners still had the right to graze cattle in open areas of the Forest, although the numbers wandering around decreased a lot after the War. I don't remember that many cattle in Loughton, except for some alongside Epping New Road and on the Rangers Road near Connaught Waters although, after I began driving in 1960, I noticed many houses and blocks of flats in Woodford that were protected by cattle grids. That was rather a danger zone, as if you hit a cow it seemed to be considered your fault, even if it jumped on your bonnet.

Prior to about 1960, when the forest deer were herded into their sanctuary created at Theydon Bois, we would often glimpse the shy creatures, particularly in the thickets between Epping New Road and Woodridden Hill. In the late 50s there was a heated debate about what should be done about the white stag of Epping Forest, an albino I suppose, which appeared mysteriously and was around for a few years until the start of the 60s. It was decided to shoot it in case it corrupted the forest's fallow deer herd, but we were all relieved that there was such a fuss made that the instruction was cancelled. The pity was, it met a sad end anyway, as it was found dead from shotgun wounds, somewhere near the Wake Arms. Although the deer are mostly in the sanctuary, some are still loose, particularly very early in the morning, near that same spot. As my late neighbour almost wrote his car off hitting a deer between the Wake Arms and the Robin Hood, I still take special care on that stretch of road.

Of course the forest was also provided ideal opportunities for courting couples who may have had no privacy elsewhere, both down secluded woodland paths, but also, in quiet parking spots, perhaps even the not so quiet gravel car park

Gradually, partly because car ownership grew rapidly, taking people further afield, by the end of the 60s there were less people in the forest, although High Beach itself seemed an exception, managing to stay busy into the 70s and beyond. It was often very difficult to find a parking space, and there always seemed to be a queue at the tea hut opposite the King's Oak. The other tea-hut, at the first junction on the way to High Beach from the Robin Hood, has always been heavily used and this tiny shed, for as long as I remember it, has remained a welcome haven, particularly for bikers and cyclists.

Loughtonians and others may drive to High Beach and Connaught Waters in reasonable numbers, but there is such a lot to see in many other parts, both on and off the beaten track. So many seem to be missing so much, and with all the excellent improvements the City of London has made to the forest it would be nice to see more advantage taken of the wonderful asset on our very doorstep.

7 Counting our chickens – The Loughton Poultry and Rabbit Club

Some Loughton residents, particularly newer ones, may not be much fussed about chickens but they might be surprised at the contribution backyard hens made to our hard-pressed wartime and post-war town. For about 11 years from 1946 they were a significant part of family life at 73 Smarts Lane.

Even though many farm workers were still away from home, egg production in Britain at the end of the war was almost the same as in 1939, thanks to ordinary people with a little bit of ground at the back of the house where hens could scratch away happily. I believe at the end of the Second World War well over one-third of British eggs were being laid by garden chickens.

During the war many Loughton residents, including some from the upper classes, kept a few hens, even though prior to the outbreak of hostilities such an activity was somewhat frowned upon by many wealthier folk, their opinion being that, in normal circumstances, it was rather *infra dig*. When peace was finally restored most of them quickly got rid of their birds, but many of us in Smarts Lane, Forest Road and other working-class roads still kept them, carrying on what we had been doing for a long time before the war started. After all, egg rationing went on until 1952, and they were expensive!

It wasn't only chickens as during the war a number of our neighbours, especially older residents, or wives whose husbands were serving in the Forces, were also breeding rabbits for meat and quite a number continued after 1945. As mentioned earlier, after the war ended, with Epping Forest cleared of dangerous materials, illicit rabbit netting also augmented certain Loughton larders, but that only lasted several years before being halted by the deadly myxomatosis. Thankfully, we didn't hear of any case of the disease infecting Loughton's domestic rabbits.

As well as satisfying a common need, a camaraderie developed among some of the keener poultry and rabbit keepers, further stimulated in those hard times by a wish to pay less for feed, to learn the best ways to use household scraps for chicken food and how to deal with any poultry problems. Most of the food pellets, grain and supplements such as grit, fish and bone meal, used to be bought from Goulds, the corn merchants on the site of Morrison/Safeway, and while this highly reputable family business no doubt charged reasonable prices, they had to make a profit and were in a monopoly position.

So, as an alternative after the war a group of Loughton poultry keepers, including my father, rejoined the non-profit-making Loughton Poultry and Rabbit Club, which had been active since the 30s, and which survived into the 50s, using the very large hut that used to stand between 39 Smarts Lane, the end-terraced house of Street's milk roundsman, George Hockley, and the wide gravel path at the back of the High Road police station, which still runs alongside No 31, the next house. Even now, Smarts Lane has no Nos 33 to 37. The hut is no longer there, having stood empty for some years after the club closed down. It was demolished some time before the old mid-19th century police station was scrapped in 1963, making way for what is still the rear entrance to the car park of the current one, a truly unpleasant building which opened in 1964.

The hut was behind a high slatted fence with a heavily padlocked gate, and it would open up at 7 o'clock every other Wednesday evening for members to meet, enjoy a chat and buy their supplies, which came direct from small Essex producers. Everything was stored in large covered bins

34

around the walls and also on sturdy shelves members had built themselves. As quite a number of Loughtonians around us, including Old Harry, kept pigeons, the club also did quite well selling maize for them and as a sideline it also sold flower and vegetable seed.

It was a cosy place with a comfortable agricultural smell, and on a table in the middle were past copies of *Poultry World* and *Farmers' Weekly*, and around it a few old kitchen chairs. Only club members could buy supplies, but subscriptions were minimal, and you could join and purchase on the same evening. Orders would be scooped into strong paper bags or sometimes into small sacks members had brought along, then weighed and the price written on a ticket to be given to one of the wives stationed behind a small cash register.

Although I can't remember the names of the club's officials, I do recall that one or two on the committee were, perhaps surprisingly, quite well-to-do professional class Loughtonians who enjoyed poultry keeping purely as a hobby. The committee only met when they felt the need, but proper minutes were kept, and there was an Annual General Meeting with a formal election of officers. I wish I could see some of those records.

My father was on the committee for a time, and the club played a large part in his developing quite a productive sideline. Our garden at No 73 was a reasonable size so, like his father, Old Harry, Dick had built a small hen-house with a run surrounded by strong chicken wire, in which were a dozen of probably the most popular hens at the time, Rhode Island Reds, very sturdy, hardy birds. Contrary to most people's perception of chickens, I found them quite sociable birds although, for poignant reasons, I soon realised that it was upsetting to become too attached to them. However I did keep an exceptionally tame cock bantam for several years, before he finally died peacefully of old age.

Those original hens, from the age of about six months, were excellent layers, and I enjoyed collecting the eggs, often from under the sitting birds. My father would give some away to hard-up neighbours, but soon realised the potential to expand a little. After sounding out possible customers in the Lane, Forest Road, Eaton Bros and in Forest Hall (more of which elsewhere) at the end of High Beech Road, now an Evangelical Church, and where he helped out as part-time caretaker, he decided to expand his little business.

We kept the original hen house and run, but managed to find enough wood to build two more sheds without runs where we would rear day-old chicks, as well as enclosing a further area for when they became semi-adult pullets, still leaving room for a small vegetable and flower garden. My father wired up the sheds so that the day-old chicks could be kept warm in large incubators that he built entirely himself, heated from the top by bulbs set in big round reflectors. He also made all the water and food troughs, keeping everything scrupulously disinfected to keep his little flock free from red mite and coccidiosis, both common infestations, and feeding them on home produced food.

Their main diet was a home-made mash of ground baked bread and boiled potato peelings, with bone or fish meal added, plus separate troughs of wheat or fowl pellets, with grit for developing strong eggshells. Making that staple fare was quite a tedious process and my mother, although she always helped, took rather a dim view of it. The bread was baked in our Nichols and Clarke grate, pushed through a mincer screwed to the kitchen table, the handle mostly turned by me, before my father mashed the whole lot together in a bucket outside. Hard work but the hens thrived on it.

The chicks came in boxes of up to 50, mainly Rhode Island Reds, but also some Light Sussex, all very healthy. As they had plenty of air-holes it was almost unknown to find a dead chick in the boxes, and they were soon running around safely, rapidly growing big and strong enough to be moved to the outside runs, before finally being sold.

We always kept enough back to satisfy our egg customers, selling the rest, some at about six weeks old, some almost ready to lay, others for the table. Most of the latter, including some fattened-up cock birds, left us just before Christmas, plump and tender, and Young Harry, my father's brother, with his past experience as a butcher, would deal with all the nasty side. I know I could never have been a farmer as I always felt so sorry for them when they went.

Our regulars would come from all over the local area to collect their birds, and my cousin Maureen reminded me that, for some years at Christmas my father would take about half a dozen of the biggest oven-ready ones, free of course, to the Bethnal Green branch of the family, where money was really tight, and from there my Aunt Marie would distribute them to my mother's other East End relatives.

Dick's little cottage industry, with over 300 birds bought, reared and sold in one year, reached its peak in 1952, my last year at Staples Road School, although he still did well until around 1954, before a combination of restrictions on domestic poultry keeping plus cheaper eggs and chickens in the shops, as well as the end of rationing, sent it into sharp decline.

Another nail in the backyard hen coffin was the little lion which, from 1957, courtesy of the Egg Marketing Board, buyers wanted to see stamped on their eggs. Our little enterprise at 73 Smarts Lane finally ended very tamely in that year, when I went with my father in a borrowed car to a poultry farm near Maldon to pick up our last ever day-old chicks. There were only 50, and when they were gone we dismantled the sheds, and made the runs into lawns and flower beds.

Much had changed over those 11 years, and most Loughtonians had given up on chickens long before my father and few of our neighbours bothered any more. The Poultry and Rabbit Club's membership had dropped away sharply and it was wound up in the early 50s, a few years before my father finally gave up chicken rearing, but during its brief existence its aims had been achieved, especially as far as our family was concerned. Although my mother was very relieved when it was all over, you have to remember that, for several austere years after the war chicken was still a real treat, so Dick's little business, in its own small way, had served a useful purpose.

I learned a lot about chickens and always had a very soft spot for them so I was sad to see the decline of the backyard hen in the 50s and 60s. Chickens seemed to enjoy their lives just after the war, scratching about contentedly, producing about 120 eggs a year, a figure which almost doubled by the mid-60s, although by then most hens were housed in cruel cramped cages. It's even worse now, chickens produce over 300 eggs each year, but when any hen's output tapers off, it is sent straight to the pet food factory. When Dad started in 1947 free range hens, including millions in gardens like ours, produced almost all British eggs. By the time he gave up it was under 20%, dwindling almost to nothing by the end of the 60s. Now, with a revival in free range and the enthusiasm for organic production, there has been something of a recovery and long may it continue.

Like others in the Lane, we also kept rabbits. My favourites were Buck, a big dark brown lad, and a lighter female, Sandy. She was also large and produced numerous litters and I used to wonder, before I learned a few simple facts, where they all came from. We kept our rabbits in cages next to the ferrets but, strangely enough, they never seemed to be aware of their deadly neighbours. When Sandy died, we gave up the rabbit side-line, although for some years I kept a black and white Dutch one as a pet which, showing a woeful lack of imagination, I named Dutchy.

The Poultry and Rabbit Club held several open days in the hut and a few small shows, and in one of those Dutchy won the 'best in show' cup. Rabbits are not notably bright, but I fitted a cat collar and lead on her, and she would follow me, perhaps helped by a few gentle tugs, down Smarts Lane to Nan and Granddad in No 45.

Perhaps the highlight of the Club's existence was the Grand Rabbit Show it staged for the 1951 Loughton Fair, an all-day event with entries from all over England.

Apart from our dog, Floss, and various cats, rabbits and ferrets, the only other animals we looked after turned up totally unexpectedly. Late one evening Floss was barking furiously round the back of one of the huts. I went out and looked into a recently made hole that went underneath, in time to see a large hedgehog scurrying off. My father shone a torch into the hole, and there, to our astonishment, was a nest of baby hedgehogs. As they couldn't get at the chickens or their eggs, they were doing no harm so, apart from leaving them regular saucers of water and scraps, we left them alone, kept Floss indoors and after a few weeks, they had gone. For such small animals, hedgehogs cover considerable distances every night, so we liked to think they made it to the forest. As there were a lot less cars then, they probably did.

By the time people in Smarts Lane and other roads stopped keeping chickens recovery in Loughton was well under way and, looking back, I like to think that the end of our domestic poultry keeping meant that a very tough period in the town's life was behind us. So I still think of the little club when we drive down the Lane and look at the big rear gates of the police station and the high brick wall bearing the sad prominent notice warning everybody that the area is covered by CCTV cameras. Gone are the days when you could leave your bike outside the Poultry Club, as we used to call it, for the whole evening and it would still be there when you came out.

8 The London County Council Debden Estate

In 1945, when building of the LCC Debden Estate began on open land north-east of Loughton, I don't suppose I even realised it was under way. I'm told there were comments, sometimes subdued, but certainly not always, that this would be a threat, that Debden would simply become an imported slum, but I was too young to take much notice. Funny though, I certainly recall that, later on, reaction had turned completely the other way, and there was jealousy, quite a lot in fact, because the Debden dwellers had nice new houses, not slums at all, while many Loughtonians still lived in their small, unmodernised terraces.

I do remember a fair amount of the years from about 1948, when the influence of the rapidly growing Debden Estate was being felt in the rest of Loughton. You don't add 40 or so new roads, more than 4,000 houses and about 15,000 newcomers in less than 10 years without some problems, especially when shopping facilities didn't keep pace with the growing population. Add in the fact that much food, even bread for a time, was still rationed in the post-war 40s, into the 50s for some items, so shoppers from Debden, buying from Loughton retailers, were aggravating those shortages. Sad to say, you then had a recipe for resentment and, even at that young age, I was conscious of it.

Also, at the same time, building was going on in what I knew as the River Estate, that is the council area (developed not by the LCC but by Chigwell UDC) behind Loughton Way, on the Buckhurst Hill borders, part of which faced, and was sometimes flooded by, the River Roding. There was a bit of a hiccup there, as some of the houses around Bradwell Road and, on the Buckhurst Hill side, Boxted Close, where my cousin Maureen lives, were, in 1948, because of the flooding, being boarded up as fast as they were being built. Dried out, they were eventually mainly taken up by ex-servicemen, provided they could guarantee being able to meet the 25s. weekly rent.

Then there were the prefabs, disparagingly named 'little matchboxes', along and in turnings off Oakwood Hill. The prefabs were in fact the first part of the Debden Estate to be built.

38

Although there were a few basic shops in Oakwood Hill, Pyrles Lane, Valley Hill and at the Roding Road crossroads, all this rapid development added to the scarcities at the High Road retailers. It was a long time, maybe eight or nine years, before Debden Broadway was fully up and running, thus largely relieving the pressures on Loughton.

In the Loughton of around 1947–48, particularly in the High Road, most faces were at least familiar to me, even if I didn't know the names, but that soon began to change. I can well remember when I was six or seven, when walking round the village on Saturdays doing errands on my own, as was quite normal for children at the time, that I started to see more and more people I hadn't seen before. On Saturdays many people from the early estate roads such as Barfields would come down Traps Hill into the town with empty prams or pushchairs, do their shopping, and trudge back up the hill with their purchases loaded onto them. It was quite a steady stream so of course, I wasn't the only one to notice, and the newcomers became an increasingly frequent topic of conversation.

Compared with many from the town, some estate dwellers, often from very tough backgrounds, sometimes had a more extrovert way about them and there were some rather intolerant Loughtonians who were selective about who they mixed with. It worked the other way as well, as there were people from Debden who, because they felt such people were making them unwelcome, did not settle easily into their new homes. I am not suggesting that bad feeling was general, that wasn't the case at all, but even into the 50s there certainly was a discernible measure of vexation.

Because my mother was an East Ender born and bred, she felt total sympathy with the Debdenites, as I remember many of our townsfolk calling them, pointing out that they deserved better, many having either been blitzed out of their homes, or having lived in dire circumstances in the East End. She would make a point of starting a conversation with the people who had so much in common with herself, and I would stand by listening. I'm reminded by Maureen, that, even so soon after the War, some people found it too easy to forget that many of those being re-housed were heroes returning from the fighting, but who had no homes when they got back.

We knew a number of her old friends, and there were relatives too, rehoused on the Debden or Hainault Estates, in the Oakwood Hill prefabs as well. Although on the one hand they appreciated their good fortune, many Londoners, even though they had been living in grim conditions, genuinely felt a great sense of loss of community. On the other side of the coin, there were many my mother knew, including her sister Marie, who spent years on the waiting list for rehousing and became extremely frustrated by the endless bureaucracy of the points-based selection system.

Mrs Jean Barnford, a good East End friend of my mother, lived with her husband and daughter in a prefab on the corner of Barncroft Close and Oakwood Hill. She, like lots of others, was there for many years longer than she had been led to expect, only leaving when theirs was finally demolished at the end of the 60s. I remember visiting there several times, and thinking the inside was a lot better, for instance, than my grandparents' tiny terrace in Smarts Lane. A major upside of prefabs was that you could erect them in a few hours, but the downside included bad condensation, and that part of the construction was with asbestos sheeting – whether or not it was the most dangerous sort, I'm not sure.

Later, at Buckhurst Hill County High School, where I started in 1952, at least half of my close friends, and of the boys in the school football and cricket teams I played for, were from the new estate. But it wasn't all a bed of roses for them. Probably, of the seven or eight Debden families I got to know well, most of the wives still had to supplement the weekly income. This would be about 1954, and even then, as there was still the demand, and as they could only take on part-time work, many would augment their funds by cleaning in larger Loughton houses.

I don't know any figures showing to which secondary schools children from the respective parts, Debden Estate or otherwise, went on in, say, 1952 when I left Staples Road. By that time the local extensive primary and secondary school building programme to cater for the newcomers, which began about 1948, was virtually complete and, added to Buckhurst Hill County High and Roding Road Secondary Modern, both built in 1938, there was probably enough choice of local free schooling, plus the fee-paying options. So, in theory, most children, whether estate dwellers or from the old town, had the opportunity to find their level. Whether it was the proper one or not depended hugely on the dreaded 11-plus, more of which later.

One important question is, after initial teething troubles, did all of us, brought together so abruptly, end up with the same chance of sharing in the national recovery that began gradually in the 50s? Although money and connections still mattered, and there was certainly a great deal of both in some parts of Loughton, the playing field was levelling off for most of us, and from the 50s and beyond, Loughton's prosperity owed much, not simply to national recovery, but also to the enlarged customer base and pool of talent that was transplanted alongside the old town back in the mid-40s.

9 Staples Road and other schools

Staples Road School is wonderfully located on sloping ground only a few yards across the road from Epping Forest and apart from a rather bleak utilitarian canteen building added well down the incline in the late 40s (and now scheduled for demolition) it still looks like a nineteenth century village school. The rest of Staples Road is also almost completely unspoiled so the whole aspect remains pleasing to the eye.

From when it opened in 1888, until my time in the infants and juniors, that is, the mid-40s to the early 50s, Staples Road School played a huge part in Loughton life. After the Second World War it was still the town's only junior school and children from above and below the railway line were in its extensive catchment area, as were some children from the new Debden estate up to about 1948, since final completion of St Nicholas County Primary in Borders Lane had fallen behind schedule. There was a small infants' school, St Michael's, at the bottom of Roding Road, but at age seven pupils had to transfer from there to Staples Road.

Staples Road School obviously remains important to the Loughton of 2006, but the early 50s building of new state infants and junior schools (Alderton and White Bridge County Primary Schools) reduced its relative significance from then on. Because I went there I have focused on Staples Road, but the new junior and secondary schools made big contributions to the district in the rest of the 50s, the 60s and beyond.

As far as I know, immediately after the War there were no playgroups or nursery schools in Loughton, so the shock of day one at Staples Road Infants School in September 1945 was too much for some children, and I can clearly remember some harrowing goodbyes at the school entrance. I started there soon after recovering from the measles, and although I enjoyed my time in both the infants and the juniors, until I left in July 1952, my initial meeting with my first teacher, Mrs Miles, was also a little embarrassing. When she met my mother and me at the school entrance, she was told about the measles, but that I was clear of any infection. She was still worried I might pass it on, so my mother had to open my shirt and lift up my vest to prove that all my spots had really cleared up. After that, though, all was well, and my enjoyable years there had begun.

The hall had dividers that could be folded back to make extra space for the children to put on small plays and concerts and the desks were old fashioned wooden ones with inkwells, but we had to use pencils at first. We used pens in the first year of junior school, and the old inkwells were filled by monitors from older classes, but soon after that they were no longer used, as we were asked to provide our own fountain pens and bottles of ink. Apparently the older iron desks were sold off, some to pupils of the time, but I don't remember that happening.

There was an obvious early attempt to assess our abilities, as one thing I remember in our very first week was having to solve a little book of simple mazes within a very short time, before handing it back to the teacher. Presumably that was our first-ever IQ test. Other regular assessments followed in what seemed to be a continuous streaming process that also determined where you sat in the class, brighter pupils near the front, weaker ones further back. Class work was openly competitive; from the very start we knew our positions in every subject, and everything we did earned us stars of various colours up to gold, depending how we performed. I have heard comments about 40s and 50s pupils being ruled by fear of physical punishment but, apart from having to watch out for occasional chalk or blackboard duster missiles, my recollection of my Staples Road years is that we did as we were told out of respect, not fright.

In all my time at Staples Road I went home for lunch, so my comment about school dinners is indirect – perhaps the kindest opinion I have heard is that they were unexciting. When I started in the infants a few of us would walk home at lunchtime, unaccompanied by parents, back to our houses in Staples Road itself, Forest Road, and Smarts Lane. How it happened at first, I'm not sure now, but we became friendly with a young German POW in a peaked army cap who used to chat to the Staples Road residents, and he would walk along with us. He was probably on forest clearing duties, and based either at Lippitts Hill, or near the LNER sports ground behind Loughton Station. He would leave me at our gate but one day my father came back for lunch as well, and saw me with him. There was no animosity or unease and although the war had ended only a few months earlier, as the German's English was good, my recently demobbed father had the first of several very friendly conversations with his erstwhile enemy. Although we knew him for several weeks I can't recall his name; one day he simply wasn't there, so I suppose he had at last been allowed home.

I remember more about years two and three, when Miss Jenkins, whom we adored, was our teacher. It was probably as early as the second year in the infants, that is maybe even four years before the exam, that our parents were told if their child had a chance of passing the 11 plus, and from then many of us felt the pressure of expectation. I still have a photo taken in my last term in the infants, showing Miss Jenkins and her 40 faithful devotees, most of whose names I remember. I also have a junior school class photo without our teacher, Mr Reece, but with most of the same pupils, three years older, some of whom were smiling less, maybe because we were about to split up and move on to new schools, or perhaps they were wondering if they were among the lucky 20% that normally made it through the 'scholarship' as many parents called it. In fact, studying that photo now, I believe that 14 or 15 out of our class of 39 passed. Of those, eight were boys who went on to Buckhurst Hill County High. Although that seems a much higher ratio than that normally given as the success rate, we should not forget that if results from pupils not in the 'A' stream are included, the success ratio is obviously a great deal lower.

I believe that just over half the pupils in that old class photo lived 'above' the railway line, the rest below, and that six came from Smarts Lane or Forest Road. I am almost certain that, apart from one who lived in Alderton Hill, none was from the wealthiest roads, such as Connaught Avenue, Traps Hill or Ollards Grove, so I suppose children from such roads were mainly privately educated, many, in the case of boys, at St Aubyns in Woodford, or for the girls, City of London School.

When the 11 plus was over, and we knew the results, Mr Reece decided we needed some light relief, so he obtained permission to take pupils in his class who were interested in football to his house in York Hill, to watch England versus Austria on his television. There was a good crowd there, although the result, a 2–2 draw, was a little disappointing.

In one way I'm absolutely certain the newly built Loughton schools were an improvement on Staples Road. They no doubt had decent indoor toilets. When I was at Staples Road, and for years after I left, the lavatories were truly horrendous. The junior loos, girls and boys, were housed in blocks right at the bottom of the playground, often smelling badly in the spring and summer, and frequently freezing up in the winter, especially in the spectacular snows of 1947 and the prolonged frosts of 1962–63. I remember boys in the infants having to use the junior boys' toilets outside, but I believe infant girls were allowed to use inside toilets near the cloakroom. Some children in the infants were obviously shy or simply too late in asking to be excused, as there were a number of mishaps, necessitating being cleaned up and sometimes a partial change of clothes, which was why spare underwear was kept in one of the school cupboards.

It was in those toilets that I learned very early from the older boys that only cissies tucked their shirts inside their pants, and there were several lads who were ribbed about that – those garments also defined which playground gang you could join. Boys with elastic topped pants looked down on those who wore the baggy ones with loops for braces – there was a similar gang divide over the belts or braces question, and peer group pressure was intense to own one of those brightly striped elasticated belts that fastened by snapping together a pair of metal curled snakes.

We were teamed off into 'houses' – St George, St Andrew, St David (mine) and St Patrick for events like sports day, or dreadful country dancing competitions. Sports day was normally held in the playground and, wearing our appropriately coloured cotton team bands, we all had to compete in the heats, but only the final placings scored points. While I was there sports day was also held in the forest, once on the Stubbles, but only once, as far as I recall, and also on Drummaids, again only the one time. As both seemed much more enjoyable days than those held within school grounds, I'm not sure why we had to use the playground rather than the forest, but it may have been something to do with the Corporation of London being unhappy about it.

The forest was a bonus and was really an extra classroom for nature studies as well as an extended playground. In my time at Staples Road, and much later, pupils were allowed into the forest at lunchtime, but had to keep the school building in sight. Not everybody obeyed that instruction, but threats to withhold the privilege kept most in order. Sometimes the bell in the turret would be the summons to return to our classrooms, or lunchtime duty teachers or helpers would cross Staples Road and into the forest, ringing hand-bells to speed up the process.

Country dancing, which most of the boys and many of the girls hated, was a regular weekly summer lesson in the playground, or on the forest clearing opposite the school and Staples Road used to put on displays for parents and enter teams in district competitions, although I can't remember if we ever won anything. Apart from the two mentioned earlier, the only other Staples Road photo I have is of our 1952 football team that won the Forest Division Schools Cup, which included teams from schools in Chigwell Urban District, Chingford and Woodford. That was a really big event for us, and the school allowed a large number of older pupils to watch the final against Woodford Green, played at Chigwell Primary's ground – Dennis Brown and Bryan Mowles scored the goals in our 2–1 win. Some Loughtonians may remember Bryan, who lived in Meadow Road, as being a truly exceptional local sportsman. Sadly, he died while still a fairly young man. I am told the cup is now in Staples Road School – presumably they were the last winners before the Forest Division ceased to exist.

As mentioned elsewhere, we had swimming lessons at the freezing open air High Beach pool – we normally went there and back on foot, although eventually a coach was laid on, even though we could walk it in less than 40 minutes. I'm not surprised that that pool closed in the 50s, as it was grubby, with cracked tiles and in desperate need of what is now called a makeover, but in the mid-60s Loughton Pool was built at the bottom of Traps Hill. Although I haven't seen it, I understand that the pool is now being used again, presumably by customers of the Kings Oak, which advertises a swimming pool among its facilities.

We had regular lectures about road safety, and cycle proficiency lessons were held in the playground by the Road Safety Officer, Sergeant Murray, a tall man with a moustache, based, I believe at Loughton Police Station, as he could also be seen around the town. I didn't own a two-wheeled bicycle until I went to Buckhurst Hill County High, so I didn't join in, but those who did and passed the final tests held at Roding Road School were awarded badges and certificates.

We had early lessons on thrift and to back those up were encouraged to buy savings stamps every week that were then stuck into small books to be taken to the Post Office when they were full, so that a proper account could be started for you.

Apart from our daily one-third of a pint of milk, while we were in the infants we were also given free orange juice and, if you could stand it, a big spoonful of cod liver oil and malt. Most of my classmates loved it, but I thought it was ghastly stuff. The teachers said it was full of vitamins that would keep us healthy, so it was a big shock when, one morning we were gathered together to be told that one of the girls in my class would not be coming to school for a while as she was terribly ill, and that we should pray for her. Some weeks later, how long I don't know, it was announced that she was much better now, but that she would still need all our love. She was a victim of infantile paralysis, polio, and when she came back one of her legs was in an iron and leather brace. Thankfully, she was the only Staples Road child I can remember who suffered in that way.

44

We had regular health checks in both the infants and juniors, but mainly the former. We would line up for the 'nit nurse' who would sit us on a wooden chair, while she bent our heads forward, peering closely to see if we were infected with lice, before inspecting our hands, front, back and fingernails, then our necks. I'm sure there were cases of pupils with nits, but I honestly cannot remember a single one, so perhaps any unlucky child's parents were told in confidence later on.

The dentist was a completely different proposition. A classroom would be set aside for the visit, and we would line up, hoping against hope that our names would not be put on the list for a trip to the school dentist's surgery in the health centre in Buckhurst Way, near the Monkhams pub. If, after the inspection, you had to go there, and most did, we waited in dread, as we had all heard grim tales about the place. Based on my own experience, those accounts were probably true as the only time I went there I saw some children who, because they could hear screams from those suffering in the chair, were already shrieking as they were dragged from the waiting room to the surgery.

We had thorough medicals at Buckhurst Hill County High, with dental checks on the same day, but if our teeth needed treatment, we were able to go to our own dentist, provided we returned with confirmation that we had been, something that became an option in my final years at Staples Road. I have talked to friends who were educated privately from 5 to 11, and they all tell me that their schools were never visited by any nurse or dentist. I'm not sure what to conclude from that.

Staples Road pupils contributed to Loughton life through concerts at Lopping Hall, and joined in church services, mainly at St Mary's. One Christmas, probably 1949, I was one of the readers – the text was Luke 2:1 to 7, and a year or so later we presented a nativity play at St Mary's when I was a lowly shepherd, and had to walk behind the three Wise Men as we approached the manger. Mary was supposed to turn round and gaze in awe at the approaching procession, but something comical must have caught her eye, as she began giggling and shaking, which rather undermined the solemnity of the presentation of gold, frankincense and myrrh.

It is axiomatic that in the 40s and 50s Staples Road School existed, as it still does of course, to educate, and despite classes of around 40, all the teachers I remember did their best to do that. However it was very obvious for most of our time there, that our primary goal was to pass the 11 plus, and for at least our last two years that seemed to be the most important thing in our lives, as the incentive of a free grammar school education if you passed was still massive, even though it had been adopted from the early 30s in Essex.

Most of what we had to learn at Staples Road had already been covered by the end of the second year in the juniors, and after that the final year was largely spent doing practice maths, English and intelligence test papers for that dreaded exam. I was full of optimism at the time, but now I can imagine how it must have felt if you or your parents really knew your chances were poor, or worse. When it was over, and we knew the results, there were seriously angry reactions from some parents whose children had missed out. Those who hadn't made it mainly went on to the Brook Secondary Modern School in Roding Road, now demolished.

Later, walking down Smarts Lane to the Crown bus stop in my new navy blue Buckhurst Hill County High blazer and cap, I would meet friends on their way to Roding Road who clearly thought I had become 'stuck up' but nothing was more untrue. I was simply embarrassed, as it seemed more of a stigma to have passed than failed. Those difficulties soon faded.

The mid-40s to the end of the 60s were years like no others before, and possibly since, for education, although secondary schools in Loughton and nearby were affected less than some other areas. By providing such a valuable prize to successful candidates the 11 plus had a huge effect on how we at Staples Road were taught, creating a highly competitive atmosphere but, by the end of the period much focus was on its unfairness, and the idea of comprehensive education began to take hold. In the period we are looking at Essex retained selection and there were some excellent selective schools around our district. Choices available to boys included Leyton County High, Sir George Monoux; the mixed South-West Essex Technical School in Walthamstow, and Tom Hood in Leytonstone and, but without doubt the main goal for Loughton boys who passed was to make it to Buckhurst Hill County High, now a Sikh independent school. From 1965 the now outstanding Davenant Foundation School became available as well, although in the early years in its new Debden location it had to struggle to establish its reputation.

For girls Loughton County High School, now the mixed Roding Valley High, was probably first choice, or perhaps Woodford County High. I'm not sure if the system was fair or not, as later in my City life I met many people, colleagues and competitors, who had failed the 11 plus but whose careers were very successful, some exceptionally so. The 'remove' form at Buckhurst Hill County High, 'resit' pupils who achieved selection two years later, at 13, also produced many high achievers.

For those unlucky with the 11 plus or the entrance exams for the local public schools, Chigwell and Forest, or Bancrofts (then a direct grant grammar school) but whose parents opted to pay for a grammar style education as an alternative to that offered by a secondary modern school, there was Loughton School, known locally as the 'red cap' school. For many years, right up to the Second World War, this had been the first choice of many upper-class Loughton parents. For over 100 years, until it was demolished in the 1990s, it stood on the site now occupied by Salcombe Rise, adjacent to what is now Homecherry House, next to the Union Church. The school's name is perpetuated through the nationally prominent Old Loughtonians Hockey Club, although this is now completely open to all.

Buckhurst Hill County High School, after only 51 years, finally closed in 1989, the same year as Loughton County High School for Girls. I was, and still am, very sad about that, but at least the energetic Old Buckwellians Association is thriving, and so far over 80% of the 4825 pupils who attended the school have been traced. Loughton County High would have celebrated its centenary in 2006, and its Old Girls' Association has plans for a fitting commemoration.

I enjoyed Buckhurst Hill County High every bit as much as Staples Road, and it enabled me to make life-long friends and to pursue an enjoyable career, as well as being a stepping stone to nearly 40 years playing competitive cricket, football and hockey in Loughton and other parts of Essex. Year-by-year details of what it was like there are outside the ambit of this book, although I will end the subject of Buckhurst Hill County High by getting off my chest a long-term grievance about my journey to the school. Pupils whose bus journey to the stop outside the school gates was three miles or more received a free pass. My designated bus route was the 167, and the stop chosen to fix the starting point was by the Crown, which made the journey just over 2.9 miles, so no pass. We appealed to be allowed to choose the previous stop, by St Mary's Church, which would have been a little over the required 3 miles, but that plea was rejected by some bureaucrat in Holly House, then the local education headquarters – now a private hospital. The upshot was, unless it was really bad weather, for the whole of my seven years at Buckhurst Hill, I did the journey by bike.

10 Filling our time in the 40s and 50s

Young Loughtonians probably find it hard to imagine life without the Internet, Sony Playstations, handheld computer games, multi-screen cinemas and countless TV cartoon channels. We had none of these -- they were the stuff of science fiction, but I don't remember spending the 40s and 50s being bored. So how did my generation fill its time?

The Loughton I remember in those years, despite the tough post-war times, offered lots of leisure opportunities and, whether teenagers or much younger, we had plenty of chances to join clubs or youth organisations and many of us did.

Although television after the war was starting its second decade, it was very limited compared with now. At that time London was one of the few UK cities able to receive television broadcasts and, being so close to the capital, Loughton could benefit from the programmes, but not many of us did. Few in the town had TV sets but nearly everybody had a radio, and it stayed that way until the Coronation ignited something of a television boom.

Before then, however, my father had been one of the first in the Lane to buy a television and, remembering how it immediately attracted youngsters from the road like a magnet, what goes on these days hardly seems surprising. There weren't many daytime programmes, but there were children's broadcasts, and it was to gape at those that Smarts Lane children regularly gathered in the small back room of No 73.

With broadcast distractions so limited, entertainment or hobbies had to be self-created and that is exactly what most of us did. We had many hours in the day to fill, but kids in Smarts Lane and Forest Road always seemed able to find plenty to do outside, especially in the spring and summer months. My recollection is that there always seemed to be more outdoor activities in those two roads than anywhere else in Loughton.

Now, in an age where even adolescent children are protected so closely, are driven to and from school and rarely play outside in Loughton streets, it is hard to imagine our parents allowing us, alone or in a group with ages ranging from perhaps six to eleven, to run around Smarts Lane, or go into the forest on our own to collect tadpoles or blackberries. The only warnings we were given would be the usual ones: look both ways when you cross the road, and never to talk to strangers. Sometimes, if we took sandwiches, we would be out for most of the day.

Even if we now had as much snow in winter now as we seemed to get then, can you imagine children of eight or nine being allowed to spend hours on end on their own, sledging down Drummaids or the big slope at the very edge of town alongside Warren Hill or behind the Warren Wood pub on the Epping New Road?

There are some Loughton streets that, in the right conditions, would still be brilliant for roller skating or carting, and 50 or so years ago that is how we often used Ollards Grove, Connaught Hill, Queens Road, The Uplands, Carroll Hill and various other steep roads. We had some great races and spills were inevitable, but because cars were so few, traffic was rarely a problem. Most of the carts were home-made and Uncle Harry, my father's brother, made mine from scrap wood and old pram wheels with ropes for steering. That cart was one of the best around but like most others in the Lane, I was at a disadvantage when it came to roller skates. Those of us who had older and cheaper ones with metal wheels, useless shoe grips and no suspension were always outstripped by the lucky ones with the expensive latest style from E G Hatch in the High Road, fitted with the new rubber wheels.

We normally gathered in front of the Carpenters' Arms to play all the conventional games such as hopscotch and skipping for the girls, cowboys, cops and robbers, conkers, marbles, fivestones (jacks), flicking cigarette cards, riding bikes and scooters, but there were also a few that were more out of the ordinary.

Tipcat was popular in Smarts Lane. A piece of wood tapered at both ends was hit in the air with a stick, then struck as hard as you could as it came down. The one who could whack it furthest was obviously the winner. Very simple and very noisy.

'Queenie, queenie, who's got the ball' was a very common cry in our road. One child, with its back to the rest, would throw a tennis ball over the shoulder and one of the waiting kids had to pounce and hide it. The 'queenie' cry was bawled out in unison, the thrower would turn and point at the one with the ball, and if the guess was right first time, the one with it had to run from the Carpenters to Foster's Yard and back, a round trip of about 200 yards. Three wrong guesses, and the thrower had to run.

Because there were fewer distractions, most kids I knew used to read a lot and as Loughton was well provided with libraries, both public and private, a good book always seemed available. As well as that, with money so tight in those days, I think Loughtonians of 50 or so years ago appreciated their libraries more than they do now.

The 40s and 50s was the era of *Just William*, Jennings, Biggles and the hugely popular Enid Blyton books which, although much maligned by many critics, are still big sellers. To find as many of these as I could, from the age of about six I started going to the Loughton public library on my own. Our library was moved a few times before ending up where it is today. The first very modest one was tucked away at the back of the old Methodist Church, remaining there for some years until it was shifted to a long black-painted wooden building in Brook Road, parallel to the brook itself, alongside what were then the grounds of Loughton High School for Girls. That particular library always seemed a very welcoming place, and perhaps because its budget was more generous in those days, there was always a superb choice on the shelves. To be honest, I much preferred it to the next one, which was in The Drive, on the site of Loughton Health Centre, before finally being located in Traps Hill. Loughton's Chief Librarian in the Brook Road and, I believe, The Drive days was an impressive lady but I remember her face and helpfulness more than her name although I am fairly sure she that she went on to very senior promotion in her service with Essex County Libraries.

For a while after the war, for only a few pennies, we could also borrow books from the subscription-only Forest Library, next to the International Stores near Lopping Hall, and I occasionally used it. My mother went there more than the public library mainly because some of the books were rather more daring. The newsagents in the High Road, opposite the mechanical loo in Brook Path, is now a ladies dress shop, but for some years it housed another private library, Rose's, although we never borrowed books from there.

As was expected in those days most Loughton kids I knew in the 50s, many in the 60s as well, had at least one hobby. Many children become TV addicted or computer-literate so fast these days that it is no surprise that they enjoy their PCs or X-Boxes much more than, for example, collecting stamps. Some Staples Road classmates, although not me, would go trainspotting, now a word associated with 'anoraks'. I can remember one or two eight or nine year olds who would buy a platform ticket and spend hours on Loughton station, both in the days of steam and after 1948, when the Tube reached the town, collecting engine and coach numbers.

Staples Road School encouraged us to collect many different things and catalogue them, whether it was stamps, coins, rocks or butterflies and moths, and also to build model planes and ships and the reward for our efforts would be the inevitable coloured star. Our teachers also urged us to join the I-Spy club, which meant going round looking for birds, animals, aeroplanes, cars and many other things, and marking them off in the little books sold by the now long defunct *News Chronicle*.

In the post-war years into the early 50s, one result of the lack of TV and cars was the popularity of family walking in Epping Forest, particularly at weekends when it would be bustling. Like very many Loughtonians, we would often go for picnics in the summer and the number of people of all ages simply getting out and about in the forest was unbelievable compared with now.

Apart from those picnics, eating out in Loughton was extremely unusual, except for the occasional birthday tea in friends' houses, or family gatherings at Christmas or Easter. There were very few cafés and restaurants in the town, unlike 2006, when it is almost impossible to count the number of eating places. Even most of Loughton's pubs, more of which elsewhere, offered little other than packets of nuts or crisps, although Doris Smith in the Holly Bush, where I worked for a while, would sometimes find time to rustle up a sandwich for regular customers. It was only about 1960 that eating out in Loughton became more common.

The two High Road cafés I remember much about only did a limited day-time trade. One, rather posh, was in Hubbards, the confectioner-cum-toy shop near the Loughton Cinema, later the Century, and the other, much less refined, was Don's Café, next to the Forest Hall. The latter had been Clayden's tea-room before the war but I only knew it as Don's, although it was actually owned, I believe, by Adrian Delarue who later, probably in the late 60s, used to run the rifle and pistol shooting club at the rear of Loughton Hall.

Around 1954 to 1956 I used to call in Don's for the occasional Pepsi-Cola as it had a juke box, which I am pretty sure was the first in Loughton, as well as what I also believe was the town's first pinball machine. I remember Terry Sadler, a Laneite who worked as a painter and decorator for various local firms including Eatons, as being a real virtuoso on it, truly Loughton's own 'pinball wizard' of the mid-50s. Thanks to Terry and a few others who were sometimes able to make one sixpenny turn last almost an hour, that machine never made much money and it was eventually taken away.

Later in the 50s and 60s more High Road eating places opened up and as Don's Café was unable to compete it was eventually converted into a small garden centre, but that didn't last very long and over the years the building deteriorated badly. It has since been demolished and the site is now a Higgins development of new flats and offices, plus a toyshop.

There was another café run by Jesse Thomas at 108 High Road, next to what is now the dry cleaners at the end of Ollards Grove, and some of the Eaton Bros men used it but apart from that I know little else about it, or Jesse himself, except that he lived in Wanstead. If there were other cafés or tearooms I have overlooked, I apologise.

When it came to organised recreation, we had a lot of choice. I remember the boys' club in St Mary's Church Hall, run by Mr Warren, a stout, quite elderly man. I think his name was Bert, but to the boys he was always Mr Warren. I went there for a few years, probably from age nine to eleven, and I think we had to pay a few pence each time, which was excellent value, as we played billiards in the back room (Mr Warren did not approve of snooker, it wasn't a game fit for young gentlemen), table tennis in the main hall, board games, and we could even box. In the St Mary's hall of that time there was a small stage and he would set up a simple ring and spar with the boys. He used to wear a top denture which he would take out before sparring with us. I particularly remember John Cook, a Staples Road boy, as being a good boxer, and John Wayne (yes) from The Drive wasn't bad either. I wonder where they are now.

The Loughton Club in Station Road, to which I refer in another chapter was by the 50s, perhaps earlier, no longer a boys' club, although when founded in 1901, it was intended for both men and boys. There were probably boys' clubs run by other Loughton churches, perhaps for girls, too, although, looking back, I don't recall girls as being so well catered for.

Loughton had no shortage of the national organisations such as the Scouts, Cubs, Guides and Brownies, and my cub pack was the 41st Epping Forest which met at Loughton Union Church. There were packs in other parts of the town, for example at St Mary's, St John's and St Michael's. There were also branches of groups that were run on more military lines, such as the Air Training Corps, Army Cadets, the Boys' Brigade and the Girls' Life Brigade, but the majority of us I think, preferred to be organised in a rather more relaxed way.

Our Akela at the 41st was called Vera and she generated great enthusiasm in everything we did, so when we chanted 'We'll dob, dob, dob', in response to her 'dyb, dyb, dyb', we genuinely meant it. Sadly, I can't remember Vera's surname, but I do recall my gratitude when, having passed the 11 plus, she presented me with a Parker fountain pen that served me well at Buckhurst Hill County High, until it was stolen from my satchel some years later.

From 1949 to the end of the 60s Loughton's Scouts and Cubs would take part in national Bob-a-Job Week and I remember my reaction both to the excellent response of some residents and, in some cases, to the shameful way some really took advantage of the willing boys. The 41st Epping Forest's 'target' area included some of the wealthy roads such as Ollards

Grove, Forest View Road, Connaught Hill and Nursery Road, as well as less well-off ones like Meadow Road. It was all too clear at times that the generosity of some residents was inversely proportional to their wealth or the size of their property. Most of the time though it was an enjoyable week and there were very many who more than made up for the stinginess of the few. With some others, I left the 41st in 1954 or 1955, mainly because by then we were very involved in school or club sport. Bob-a-Job Week continued until 1970, when it became Scout Job Week, partly because some still chose to interpret the 'bob' literally and also, because the shilling had declined in value over the years, more and more jobs were not being fairly rewarded. Anyway, with decimalisation imminent, '5p-a-Job Week' would sound daft.

One of Loughton's most impressive sights was the annual parade through the town on Remembrance Sunday which was held in the post-war years before the town's commemoration of the dead of both wars, naturally enough, became an event on rather a smaller scale. In those years, when the Second World War was still very fresh in our memories, the parade would be made up of marching groups from all the youth movements, the three Services, the British Legion and various local adult organisations, all carrying large flags. A loud band, probably the Boys' Brigade, would lead the parade through the town to the War Memorial on King's Green for the commemorative service, and I remember very impressive numbers of applauding spectators, and some would join the end of the parade and follow it to the memorial. It was a unifying experience and I think most of us from all social levels felt very close as a result.

In the mid-50s many of us teenagers joined the mixed Loughton Youth Centre in Roding Road, and as well as offering many sports and other activities the LYC broadened our horizons in different ways. That was the time we were becoming more aware of trends in fashion, and taking a serious interest in our appearance. So for those of my age the Youth Centre became something of a watershed, making us see ourselves, or so we thought, through the eyes of others, especially those of the opposite sex.

This reference to the Loughton Youth Centre takes my Loughton leisure time recollections into the mid- to late 50s. From then into the 60s increasing amounts of our time seemed to be spent trying to make much more social headway by setting out to make a better impression on those around us. How we tried to do that, and how we learned some of the necessary skills and benefited from various people and places in and around the town, will I hope become clearer later in these memories.

11 Loughton leisure into the 60s

Towards the end of the 50s into the 60s the town's improving fortunes were further boosted by being so near the capital so that most of us were better off. Nearly everybody of my generation from the Lane and Forest Road, as no doubt all over Loughton, whatever they had achieved at school had, by the time they left in 1956 or 1957, found jobs without much trouble. Their options were better by then. Some I knew, particularly from Smarts Lane and similar roads might well, even a few years before the war, have settled for poorly paid service in a wealthy Loughton household. The majority now started work at 16 and, although others were encouraged into higher education, either way there was no doubt that how we chose to spend our leisure time reflected a rising optimism.

The hated rationing, having ended in 1954, was now well behind us, and what we would now call a 'feel good factor' was washing over us, and most of our parents were also making reasonable headway. So whatever their politics and whether they were professional, clerical, manual or service industry employees working locally or in the City or the West End, Loughtonians probably conceded that Harold Macmillan had a fair point with his 'most of us have never had it so good'.

As the 60s approached other ideas were also changing. By then we were much less inhibited than a few years earlier and my generation was perhaps the first to enjoy an emerging youth culture and free and easy teenage years. It isn't that that we Loughton teenagers or young adults became particularly disrespectful, but there is no doubt that by the end of the 50s the undisputed authority in school or at home was being questioned. Against this background, and heading towards the even greater freedom and attitude changes of the 60s which many older people I knew found very hard to accept, there was a strange mix in our leisure activities.

Although Loughton and the local area offered a reasonable choice of outlets for all generations as the 50s drew to a close, many residents like my parents and most of my relatives, seemed content to sit in front of the TV. Television, boosted first by the Coronation then again, after 1955 when ITV started broadcasting, was becoming their major source of entertainment. The first family I remember with ITV were the Smiths, who ran the Holly Bush where I was a regular visitor as I was very friendly with their son Alan. He also became the first of my friends to have his own car, a brand-new Mini, but it was three years after him that I was able to afford my first one.

We could go to the cinema of course. Loughton Cinema opened in 1928, changing its name to the Century in the 50s. In the late 40s and into the 50s a regular group of us used to go there as often as we could, including to the children's 'Saturday Morning Pictures' for sixpence. Those were the days of double features, plus a newsreel and a cartoon and despite the very full programme we often watched the films twice round in the same visit, but nobody seemed to mind. The Century faced competition from the Plaza in George Lane, South Woodford, which we called 'the flea-pit' and from the much bigger Majestic a few yards away on the main road. Those two, especially the Majestic, which also had a large ballroom frequented by older Loughtonians, seemed to siphon off most of the Century's patrons, and from the late 50s it fell into terminal decline, finally closing in 1963, nearly empty even on its last night, with only 40 of its 600 seats occupied. It wasn't a particularly attractive building but even so it had much more character than the dreadful shops and flats that replaced it.

Loughton's pubs were then a very big part of the town's social life, but not in the same way as now. They were places to drink, rarely to eat. Assorted customers of all ages for whom it was their main social outlet, were regular nightly drinkers, while for many younger ones, including myself, pubs were closely linked to our sports activities and were visited mainly at weekends. My group of closest friends was heavily into sport, and cricket in particular used to take up a lot of our time. After weekend cricket matches for the Old Buckwellians we often adjourned to the Mother Hubbard in Loughton Way, which was the best pub near our ground by the River Roding. Recently demolished, the Mother Hubbard has made way for yet another block of flats.

Other sportsmen in Loughton, and there were more of them then relative to the size of the town, were also regulars of local pubs, particularly the Wheatsheaf in York Hill and the Holly Bush. There was also a solid core of residents of all ages and from all social levels for whom their local was their main relaxation. When I worked in the Holly Bush, admittedly only intermittently over a period of about 18 months, night after night the same regulars would sit on their usual bar stools or armchairs. Loughton's pubs were nothing like as classless as now and old social differences often bubbled up. It was so different then as most pubs in town had a strictly separated saloon and public bar and customers knew which was the right one for them, but if they didn't they were soon told about it. While in the Holly Bush I frequently saw customers who had wandered into the saloon bar being informed, very firmly and politely, that the public bar entrance was round the corner. They nearly always went quietly, mostly very apologetic.

Quite a number of the Holly Bush's more senior patrons belonged to the Loughton Club in Station Road. Although founded in 1901 as a temperance club for men and boys there was by then no boys' club and the premises were licensed. Although never an official member I knew the place well, as in two separate periods, the first in 1956–57 then later about 1959–60, I was often allowed, with a couple of others, to use the superb table tennis room upstairs. We were playing in local leagues and were lucky enough to be coached by a then Loughton Club member, John Miller, a county standard player. I remember the 50s steward, Paddy, very well, and it was a big shock to learn, when we went along for one of our sessions, that he had passed away very suddenly.

Sometimes, with a blind eye being turned to the rules, if the Holly Bush members of the club were short of a fourth for snooker, I would be asked to make up the numbers. That was over 45 years ago, and I haven't been inside Loughton Club since.

Some of the town's more traditional enjoyments survived to the end of the 60s and beyond. It was still the age of monthly, even weekly, whist and beetle drives; older Loughtonians, particularly the ladies, used to enjoy regular sessions in St Mary's Church Hall and other churches, but it was no coincidence that, as ownership of TV sets in the town increased rapidly, the number of such events gradually died off.

For many of us, summer or winter, what we enjoyed most, well into the mid-60s were the local dances, and initially that presented something of a dilemma. Many younger Loughtonians felt that although we still wanted our social skills to reflect some of the traditional style, we also had to take on board the latest musical, fashion and leisure trends of those changing times. Not only was Victor Sylvester still going strong, they were also the early 'rock-and-roll' years, the Bill Haley, Elvis, Buddy Holly days, so local dances, which were to play a big part in our social life, were beginning to combine the old with the new. We needed to know not only how to do the waltz, quick-step and foxtrot, but also how to jive and, a bit later on, to cha-cha. We also wanted more contact with the opposite sex and the ideal place in Loughton to combine all this was Morgans' Dance Studio, our passport to the increasing number of dances in and around the town.

Vic and Joan Morgan held their studio sessions in the function hall belonging to the old Crown Hotel, which was a lovely old building with a wide open forecourt. In 1965, in one of the saddest acts of architectural vandalism that Loughton ever saw, the Crown was demolished, making way for another pub bearing that name, (although, like some other pubs in the town, that has been changed a few times since) on the corner of the unsightly combination of a small row of shops with an office block slapped on top that totally wiped out the country town appearance of the south end of the High Road.

As well as the need for somewhere for young people to learn the basics from scratch, Morgans also offered lessons for more advanced couples to hone their steps in preparation for competitive dancing. They held separate evenings for more accomplished dancers and for beginners, and we novices went there on Fridays. They started their studio around 1956 and although those Friday sessions only lasted a few years, the timing was exactly right for my generation of Loughton teenagers and, in some cases those a few years older, to learn new skills and to have the confidence to go out and use them.

Many current townsfolk probably have no idea that Morgans was even there and some readers may wonder why it takes up space in these memories but, almost more than anything else in the Loughton of the time, it was where some of us learned the best of the old and the new.

Morgan's patrons also came from further afield, and I remember a group of young people from Leytonstone, as well as boys and girls from local schools, including Forest, Chigwell, Bancrofts, Roding Road Secondary Modern, Loughton High School for Girls and Woodford County High.

They were mainly aged from 16 to 18 but others, already at work, were a year or so older.

How did we find out about Morgans? My own recollection is seeing an advertisement that was sufficiently inoffensive to allow it to be pinned up on the strictly censored Buckhurst Hill County High senior notice board. So, as the first lesson was free, some of us decided to give it a try. With nothing to lose I started going there as part of a combined fifth form/lower sixth Buckhurst Hill County High group, one of whom later became happily married to one of the Leytonstone girls. There were also two or three engagements announced within the older group and I assume they finally made it to the altar.

As this was indeed the first serious contact some of us had made with girls, and vice-versa, it was an opportunity to dress up. The girls really put on the style, looking much more adult than the boys, many of whom like me, did not yet even possess a suit. In those days Loughton girls, even if they were the same age as us boys, always seemed about two years older.

This was also well into the age of the Teddy Boys, with their long draped jackets, drainpipe trousers and supposed aggression, but the few who came along to the lessons were never any trouble, and seemed to be feeling their way like the rest of us. To digress, I don't recall Loughton having much trouble at all with Teddy Boys. There were one or two in the Lane, but they were harmless and they, like all of them had by the end of the 50s, passed into history. Their successors, the aggressive 'Rockers', who were around until about 1965, were a completely different proposition. High Beach in particular was very dangerous at times with threatening leather-jacketed Rockers on their big motor-bikes fighting it out with the neat and tidy Mods on their small Vespa or Lambretta scooters. Epping Forest drew them both like a magnet and although their fights were nothing like the large-scale troubles in Brighton and Margate, it was still really dangerous to get near them as some from both groups were quite prepared to use more than just fists, especially the Mods, many of whom were pumped up on Purple Hearts, the 'in' drug of the time. That was certainly one of my most unpleasant local memories of the 60s but at least those gangs who invaded High Beach over 40 years ago were mostly outsiders, not from Loughton.

Turning back to Morgans, there were mirrors all around the walls, and the 'Teds' probably spent as much time as the girls gazing at themselves, making sure their huge quiffs were to their satisfaction, before being worked very hard by Vic and Joan, who made sure we all concentrated on our tuition and there was no funny business going on inside or outside the hall. As well as always being dressed immaculately our instructors were totally professional, demanding and thorough in all they did. They commanded our respect and we were grateful for what they taught us in those three-hour evenings, using Joe Loss or Victor Sylvester records for ballroom sessions, and the new rock-and-roll discs for the jive.

A downside to the Morgans' studio was that a few of my friends in the Lane made it very clear that learning to dance was strictly for wimps, but I ignored all that as the rewards were well worth a little mild derision. I'm sure many Loughton teenagers did manage well enough without Morgans' lessons but for others they were the ideal launch-pad for the expanding local social scene.

So, armed with our new skills where did we go? Loughton itself only offered infrequent opportunities and, to be frank, they weren't all that inspiring. For instance there were occasional dances at the Lopping Hall but that wasn't very up-to-date at the time. So we went further afield. We didn't have to go very far. Coffee bars were in fashion in those days but as there wasn't a good one in Loughton some of us used to meet at the one round the corner from All Saints' Church in Woodford. It was there that some of the Buckhurst Hill County High boys became friendly with the girls from Woodford County High and for a while going to dances with them became one of our regular mainstays. Other local venues of the time included the then excellent Sir James Hawkey Hall in Woodford, the Memorial Hall, South Woodford, the huge Manor Hall, Chigwell, and, best of all the King's Head, also at Chigwell, for our famous Old Buckwellians' monthly dances, by far the best around. We went to packed-out trad-jazz balls at Buckhurst Hill County High, Monoux and Leyton County High and some very big ones at Walthamstow Assembly Hall, with top bands such as Chris Barber and Humphrey Lyttelton. For those with a different taste in jazz, I believe Johnny Dankworth also played there. Many young Loughtonians often went to the glitzier Ilford Palais, although our group never fancied it, and older couples to the Majestic Ballroom. I knew a number of such pairs, well into middle age, who thoroughly enjoyed that.

There was one particular area in which the Loughton of the mid-60s was very badly served. By then eating out had really taken off, and it may be hard to believe, looking at the extraordinary number of eating places in the town now, that Loughton at that time, despite its undoubted affluence, offered a very limited choice. By that time I was engaged to Sandra and like most of our close friends, we enjoyed going to restaurants, but found it necessary to go to Gants Hill or South Woodford, where there were several really excellent ones. Although a little more choice would have been welcome we would no doubt have been horrified if we could have predicted that in 2005 there would be over 30 places to choose from, along with the problems a few of them seem to attract, particularly at weekends. I'm sure there are too many now and we would be better off without some of them.

Despite that minor quibble, the 60s in Loughton were mostly good years and, apart from being careful about the occasional Mods and Rockers jousts, we rarely felt threatened, whether in the pubs, at dances or the many parties that also became a feature of the times. We enjoyed the new music, many of us were fans of the Beatles, but I don't think the town ever became a classic example of the 'swinging 60s', as it wasn't in the conservative nature of most of the residents of the time to allow that to happen. Like the most extravagant of the trendy new fashions, it was more of a West End thing that, as soon as you boarded the Central Line to come home after work, or a night out in Town, seemed to be left far behind.

12 Are you being served?

Shopping in Loughton in the 40s, 50s and, to a lesser extent, the 60s was so very different to now that, looking back, it seems almost like another world. In the earlier years, when there were few with refrigerators, housewives had to shop nearly every day for basics such as fruit, vegetables, meat, bread and milk that would not stay fresh for long in cupboards or mesh-covered pantries. My mother did her weekly Friday shop for tinned food and other non-perishables but, like most Loughtonians, for the rest she did her buying little and often. Shopping in the High Road often meant queues, and I would sometimes be sent on errands which meant standing and waiting for quite a while to be served, but everybody was used to it, it was all quite orderly, and there was normally somebody you knew to talk to. Many shops, eager for custom, would deliver to the house, very handy if you lived in the hilly parts of town or a long way from the centre, but we were lucky as little alleys took us from home to the middle of the High Road in only three minutes.

It was no use trying to shop in the High Road between one and two o'clock, as it would almost totally shut down for lunch, nor on a Thursday afternoon, early closing day, when it would be deserted; general half-day closing in Loughton lasted into the later 60s. Digressing a little, before the War there was a local football club called Loughton Thursday, whose players were employed in local shops that closed early on that day. My father, before he worked in Covent Garden, had been employed by a Loughton greengrocer, and played for that club.

Loughton, of course, now has two supermarkets, Sainsbury's and Morrison/Safeway, plus a new, since September 2005, Marks and Spencer Simply Food. There are even larger superstores only minutes away by car that can provide almost everything we need, and the little shops my parents and neighbours used mostly closed up long ago. The following list may seem a bit like trainspotting but in the 40s to the 60s, in the High Road alone (not forgetting that in those days there were fewer of us living in Loughton), I can remember (and no doubt there were others) the names of: five bakers; four butchers; four sweet shops; five greengrocers; four newsagents; six general stores; two dairies, three chemists; two wet fish shops. Apart from all these, there was a pleasing mixture of tobacconists, shoemenders, drapers, men's shops, a few cafés, toy, hardware, bicycle and electrical shops, and a few estate agents.

Where did they all go? Of course Loughton still has specialist shops in some of the above categories but, apart from estate agents, cafés and eating places, which have mushroomed, not very many. For instance, in the present-day High Road we have only three bakers (Sprays, Ingles and Greggs), one butcher, two newsagents and no greengrocer or fishmonger, although Debden Broadway is better served for such shops, and there is a top class wet fish shop at the Roding Road crossroads.

It is difficult to keep count of all the restaurants of various nationalities, bistros, wine bars, cafés, call them what you will, but it seems to be well over 30 now, with others coming, and many of these are on the sites of our old 40s and 50s retailers.

Many other notable shops in Loughton have been replaced by financial services outlets, mainly building societies, some by charity shops, and the total effect, to those who remember the High Road's pleasantly harmonious, almost country town appearance of those days, is nothing like as easy on the eye as it used to be, with many garish and tacky shop fronts and fittings, lacking co-ordination even with the next-door premises.

Although the changes I mention have taken place over nearly 60 years, many of them happened in the period we are considering in this book, namely, to the end of the 60s, and particularly in that decade itself. If you look at mid-60s photos of the High Road, apart from a few short stretches viewed from favourable angles, its appearance at that time, for example, where the old Crown stood, around Centric Parade, opposite St Mary's Church, on the site of the old cinema, along the Brooklyn Court parade, opposite Loughton Cricket Club, had already suffered from mediocre redevelopment and drab, unimaginative boxy architecture.

On a brighter note, many Loughton residents will fondly remember many of the old names, and newer residents may also be interested in them. Warnes, the very friendly outfitters near Barclays Bank, was where many local schoolchildren would be taken for school clothes and uniforms, stacked neatly in cardboard boxes on ceiling-high shelves behind the counter. I think Staples Road first had its royal blue uniform in about 1950, and Warnes sold it. It was also there that I squirmed in embarrassment when, having gone with my mother to buy my first new-style Jockey briefs, the lady assistant insisted on taking a pair from the wrapping and holding them up against me to make sure they were the right size.

Probet's, Loughton's leading men's hairdressers, was at the back of Warnes' shop, and I went there often, beginning when I was very small, to be perched on the wooden board the barbers would place across the arms of the grown-up seats when giving little children a short back and sides. Sometimes mothers held their young boy's hand, as some would start crying if it was their first haircut. Madame Pauline's, next to the old Westminster Bank, was the most popular ladies hairdresser, the name sounding, unless you knew better, like a gypsy fortune teller.

For meat and groceries many neighbours would use the Co-op, the London Co-operative Society, almost next door to Barclays Bank. They loved their 'divi' with each purchase, as that could soon mount up to a tidy sum – your Co-op number was as indelibly remembered as your telephone number is today. My mother preferred a similar shop, Williams Bros, just past Woolworths, or the larger International Stores by Lopping Hall, where the assistants were uncannily accurate at judging exactly where to slice cheese with sharp wire. For fruit and vegetables I would be sent to Gladys on the corner of the tiny alley between High Road and Forest Road, or to Howes near the Holly Bush, while highly regarded among the bakers were Warrens and Sandalls. We would buy beautifully fresh wet fish from Pearces next to the cinema or from Hortons at the end of Forest Road. Back in the 50s and early 60s I can only remember one Loughton fish and chip shop, not in the High Road, but on the corner of Valley Hill and Malvern Drive. It is now Jasmine, a Chinese takeaway.

Although Loughton had a Boots at that time, on the same site as today, the most popular chemist among our neighbours was Hutchins, by the drinking fountain, the town's oldest shop, a chemist for over a hundred years, and which now also houses Loughton's tiny post office, a far cry from the magnificent one that became The Last Post pub. Loughton Nurseries next door is about the same age, and after that is probably Bosworths the excellent butchers opposite the Uplands.

There were various drapers, including the quaint Whittles and Frank Parrott, but they closed, probably in the early 50s, leaving Ingles, Loughton's biggest, in a very strong position. This was a shop with a very large frontage, well located by the Drive, and over the years it branched out into large furniture and beds. They traded for a long time, before finally closing sometime in the 90s. Toys were sold in Hubbards, alongside sweets and tobacco, also in E G Hatch, which was really a cycle shop, but where I would also covet expensive Meccano outfits or Hornby Dublo model railway sets, for whom they acted as agents, but which were way beyond our means.

Woolworths also sold toys, but cheaper ones, little lead or tin farm animals and soldiers, plus a wide range of goods, including household and gardening equipment, seeds, shoe-mending gear and toiletries all displayed on long counters with wide aisles between them – no doubt a poor use of space, but an enjoyable place to browse around, more so than anywhere else in the High Road. From an early age I began buying Christmas presents out of my own pocket money saved from birthday cash and other tips from relatives, rather than have my name included with my parents. Woolworths was where most of them were bought and, looking back, I may have shown a certain lack of imagination as most years it would be chocolates or tins of biscuits, aprons, shaving sticks or bowls, bath cubes or salts, but they were generally well received, or so I thought at the time.

Even after 1965, when Sandra and I were married, one of my favourite High Road shops, and one we used in preference to those in Chelmsford, near where we lived at the time, was Fords, the china and glass shop almost opposite the Royal Standard. I used to think Fords had the nicest window display in the whole of Loughton and although narrow, the inside went back a long way, allowing them to carry an impressive range of stock. I don't remember exactly when another favourite, Jollys, the Art Shop, started business but I believe it was almost 70 years ago. I recall buying my first geometry set from there in 1952, when I started at Buckhurst Hill County High. It's still an excellent shop, the best place in Loughton to buy presents for creative grandchildren, and used to be the best place to find a decent birthday card. However, after such a long time in Brooklyn Parade, which was built about 1938, high rents and rates have now forced it to relocate to the other end of town, taking over the former video shop near the Holly Bush, which in earlier days had been Dennis's the well-known butchers. At the time of writing The Art Shop no longer sells cards but they tell me they may decide to stock them again – I hope so.

Sandra and I used to enjoy Ambrose's auctions and we have success-fully bid for a number of items there. We were sad to see it close down in September 2005, and relocate to Bedford. Another old link gone: who would go to Bedford? However, a new auction room, Boningtons, has now opened on the Ambrose site.

It would be easy to carry on at greater length about old High Road retailers, and many other names would certainly bring back more memo-ries to older readers, but space precludes that. However, before moving on, I will mention some other shops, but not in the High Road. These were the little traders near our house, confectioners and grocers, butchers, shoe menders and barbers, all scattered about in Forest Road, Smarts Lane, but less so in High Beech Road, every one of which is gone now.

George Grimsley and Son was tucked away near the Carpenters' Arms but, despite that, it was very well known, a great shop, the preferred butcher of many Loughtonians, from the big houses in Nursery Road and others around there, Ollards Grove, Connaught Hill for example, and from the Lane itself. The only difference among Grimsleys' customers was that most, though not all, from outside Smarts Lane or Forest Road, would have their meat delivered. Chris Pond recalls relatives from High Beach and Sewardstone who used to make the trip to Grimsleys. When I lived in the Lane, the shop was run into the 60s by Sonny Grimsley, the son of the founder, whom I knew well. I believe his first name was Horace, but he was always Sonny to adults and Mr Grimsley to children. This lovely man would take any amount of trouble over the smallest order, and was a real old-time butcher, standing in Wellingtons on his sawdust strewn floor, de-boning, filleting, rolling and stringing meat and poultry, slicing bacon or anything else his customers wanted, however fiddly, before passing it back to his wife behind him in her little hatch, calling out the price for her

61

to collect the money. Older residents may also remember Sonny's father, nicknamed 'Hookie' as he had lost an arm, in the Great War I believe. That didn't prevent him from handling even whole sides of meat by simply digging his hook in and pulling them around with that and his good hand. Grimsleys later became a cheap knick-knack shop, then a small outlet for plumbing supplies.

Another favourite was Frank Button's little sweet shop-cum-tobacconist at 12 Smarts Lane, next to the big builders C S Foster & Sons, whose workmen were good customers. Only a few feet wide, despite rationing it was stacked with intriguing sweet jars and boxes of Black Jacks, Fruit Salad and, best of all, lemonade powder. Stout little Frank would just as happily take time to measure out a pennyworth of this delicious yellow dust into a paper bag for the kids, as he would to sell 20 Weights, Woodbines, Senior Service, or packets of rolling tobacco, Old Holborn or Golden Virginia, to adults. Frank even stocked chewing tobacco which Harry, my grandfather used to use. Some of the elderly men from the Lane and Forest Road smoked pipes, some genuine briars, but a few who still used the old clay ones. There were even a few who made their own from wood from the forest, but they burned very fast and were uncomfortable, even dangerous, to use. Many in the Lane, if pushed for cash, would ask Frank to 'put it on the slate', which he would do, or even split a packet of 10 cigarettes into fives, to make it easier for his customers. One night his shop was broken into, and it was not long after that, maybe 1951, that he closed up.

Forest Road's best known general store was perhaps Withers, run by two spinster sisters until about the mid-60s, selling almost anything you wanted, including paraffin and candles, alongside food and dry goods, which sometimes absorbed the paraffin flavour. They retired in the early 60s, about the same time as Andrews, their competitor along the road, who offered a similar range. Those premises, like so many others away from the High Road, were snapped up by property developers, and are houses now, although the one opposite Andrews, is now a picture-framing shop, Frames, that has been in business for quite a few years.

Some will remember the unusual little shop, Locks I believe, at the top of Smarts Lane, with accommodation above, at the junction with High Beech Road. It had an entrance in both roads and I recall it as yet another general store, also selling sweets and tobacco, but very handy for popping into on our way to the forest. In earlier times, as Ney's Cyclists' Rest, I believe it did a good café trade with Epping Forest day trippers and cyclists. It eventually became an antique shop, before the whole building became a private house.

Something else that died in Loughton, mainly in the 60s, was the age of the calling tradesmen, those who would deliver door-to-door, or park up at strategic locations, including Smarts Lane, to let customers walk to them. In addition to the electrical shops in the High Road, we could change accumulators for our radios from the van that would call weekly and park outside the Carpenters' Arms. That disappeared quite soon after the war, as mains electricity and new technology made accumulators obsolete.

The Corona man, popular for some years in the 50s and 60s, would also park his lorry outside the Carpenters, strange really as he was competition, first for the Neals, then the Martins, the publicans who followed them. We would buy soft drinks from the driver, in large bottles with glass stoppers and a pink rubber washer, held on by thick wire, returning empties at the same time. The shrimp and winkle man would use the very same spot and he was the best of all. We, and many neighbours, would never miss the chance of the Sunday pint of prawns or shrimps, or the shiny black winkles that needed a long pin to extricate the curly meat from the shells, making sure the scaly black top was removed before you ate it. You could also buy shrimps and winkles every day in the High Road, but they always seemed to taste better from that old van.

Even into the 50s there was a knife grinder, not as before the war, on a bicycle, but in yet another van that also parked outside the pub. Strangely, in November 2005, Chris Pond spotted a knife grinder working from his van outside Diggens Court, near Kings Green. Also a relic from earlier days were the gypsies selling heather and pegs, ladies you were scared to turn away in case they hexed you. A number of older neighbours, brave souls normally, if they had said no to the gypsies, would go outside when they were gone to make sure there was no strange mark on the gatepost.

The most essential tradesmen were the milkmen and coalmen. Widely respected, Jack Street delivered our milk for years and, as his dairy was almost next door to us, I knew Jack and his roundsmen, George Hockley and Bill Carter (no relative) very well. I would often go in the back to see Robin, his horse, perhaps to look at the bottle washing machinery, or to have a chat with Jack himself, until he retired at the end of the 60s. The coalmen, including Tom Willingale, a descendant of the family who fought for lopping rights in the nineteenth century, also used horse-drawn carts, loading up from the huge piles of coal and coke in the extensive yards by Loughton Station, but many later switched over to lorries. Although they were strong men, rather fearsome with leather covering their heads, shoulders and backs, and with wide thick belts to avoid slipped discs, they were often puffing as they emptied their big black sacks into our old Anderson shelter, by then a fuel bunker.

Those were the main callers, although there were visits from the bell-ringing rag and bone man on his horse-drawn cart, and occasional attempts at doorstep selling from brush or vacuum cleaner salesmen. My mother did buy a brush or two, probably out of sympathy.

Most of those mentioned here largely ceased to trade because supermarket bulk buying, cheaper prices, and one-stop shopping tested Loughton's established retailers' customer loyalty to breaking point and beyond. I don't remember it but Kelly's Directory for 1939 lists 'Tesco Stores Ltd, grocers' at 259 High Road, which seems to have closed in 1946.

However, the first proper Loughton supermarket was Fine Fare, which opened in 1961 next to the Methodist Church. The London Co-operative Society supermarket, easily the town's biggest for many years, opened in 1962, well timed, as it was only a few weeks before Christmas. The celebrity produced for the opening ceremony, essential for such an auspicious occasion, was Kenneth More, of *Reach for the Sky* and *Genevieve* fame, and there was quite a crowd there, although I wasn't among them. At the time it was almost the biggest supermarket in the country but, ironically, although it took so much trade away from traditional Loughton shops, it closed down in 1983, its shaky profitability affected, as car shopping took hold, by its limited roof-top parking space, thus enabling Presto, later Safeway/Morrison to dominate.

Sad to say, many of the old-style retailers had probably been too generous for their own good, too inefficient to survive in the new age of rising costs and tougher competition. Larger shops had opened, High Road rents and rates were too much for them so, from the 60s onwards there was little realistic option for many of the small traders but to close their doors for the last time.

It's easy to wallow in nostalgia, to regret how much the High Road has been spoiled, or how the little shops many Loughtonians will remember with affection have vanished, but there is probably more choice now, and we have the convenience of not having to shop every day. We can have tasty take-away meals delivered, or dine out in an abundance of restaurants offering a wide choice of international eating.

It may be a matter of opinion, but it's not really the same, is it? Despite their fondness for our present-day town, there is a lot about the 50s and 60s shops that many older residents must sadly miss, even though newcomers appreciate the High Road since they can find almost anything they need there.

13 Medical care

Although change was coming, Loughtonians' access to doctors or dentists after the Second World War still depended mainly on what you could pay. If you were a very low wage-earner you could, via the state insurance scheme, see a doctor for nothing, but you were still likely to be charged for other members of the family. Unless they had made provision, for example, through a provident society, those on higher incomes normally had no choice but to meet all health costs out of their own pocket. For most people hospitals weren't free either and it was normally a case of cash in advance although some patients might get their money back later.

Of course it wasn't all bad news as many of the old lethal diseases – TB, diphtheria, whooping cough and scarlet fever, which I caught in 1947, were already in decline, and we all could expect to live longer.

Plate 2. Loughton High Road in the 1930s – almost identical in 1945 but the Gas Light & Coke Co's showroom was built on the vacant plot – later Café Rouge

Plate 3. The High Road – London Cooperative Society supermarket (almost the UK's largest at the time) – October 1965

Plate 4. The High Road, 29 June 1969 – probably still the best preserved section

Plate 5. The Gardeners' Arms, April 1965 – cottages adjacent are about 400 years old

Plate 6. Smarts Lane weatherboarded cottages – still unchanged in 1969 – number 45 is second from right

Plate 7. An almost empty Smarts Lane in 1958 – and the British School (boys)

Plate 8. The British School now – a private house – March 2006

Plate 9. Off to Southend or Clacton – author is front row, 7th from right

Plate 10. Forest Road, May 1945 – off to celebrate VE Day! Photo courtesy of Lily Austin. For participants, see the Illustrations list on page 4

Plate 11. Loughton Cinema, 1928 – later the Century – closed in 1963 with only 40 of its 600 seats occupied on its last night

Plate 12. Former site of Loughton/Century Cinema – April 1968

Plate 13. The Crown, circa 1960. Patmore Bros's garage behind

Plate 14. How the view has changed – March 2006

Plate 15. Staples Road Schools – drawn by Robert Barltrop and reproduced by permission of the *Newham Recorder*. This is the former Girls', and Infant, school of 1911

Plate 16. Staples Road School – dear Miss Jenkins' class of 1949

Plate 17. Eaton Brothers' Fordson lorry LVX 781, in Meadow Road, 1949, my father (Dick) driving

Plate 18. Victor's Handyman's Shop – 1968

Plate 19. Victor's old site in March 2006

Plate 20. Willow Cottage, Loughton High Road, during demolition – March 1967

Plate 21. The Willows, March 2006

Plate 22. The Holly Bush, 8 February, 1970 – the alley to Smarts Lane has long been closed

Plate 23. Newnham House 1962 – making way for an extensive development of flats

Plate 24. The Broadway, Debden – 28 March 1965

Plate 25. Loughton War Memorial and the King's Head (now Zizzi) – 29 April 1970

However, the cost was prohibitive enough to prevent all except the wealthy from seeking treatment if they felt unwell or if their teeth hurt. Loughton was, as now, an affluent town but still an extremely stratified one and although many had no problem in paying for medical services for their families, those in the poorer streets often had a very hard time, particularly when it came to their teeth. The reality was that people like many of those from Smarts Lane, Forest Road, Meadow Road and other less well-off parts would avoid going to the doctor or dentist simply because they couldn't afford to.

In the Loughton of that time it was particularly horrible to suffer from toothache. I have seen relatives of mine in agony, faces swollen, dabbing oil of cloves or some other temporary home remedy on the afflicted tooth which often had an abscess under it (a gumboil as my grandmother always called it), until it finally burst. If it got so bad that, whatever the cost, a visit to Mr Moser, the nearest to the Lane of the town's few dentists, was unavoidable, there was no question of a filling to save the tooth. That was too expensive, so it was summarily yanked out.

My grandfather used to pronounce: 'Teeth are a nuisance. Have the lot out and be done with it.' Fortunately that was not the perceived wisdom of the next generation, but many older Smarts Lane residents seem to have agreed with him as, having saved the money, it was round to Moser's in the High Road for a new set of dentures, made by the technician in his back garden shed. Many who lacked either the money or the courage would simply allow their teeth to loosen over the years until they finally dropped out.

There was no fluoride in Loughton's water then, people ate a lot more sugar and were often neglectful of even basic dental hygiene. Eucryl tooth powder was often used instead of toothpaste, salt was a common substitute and sometimes a strip of flannel dipped in salt would be used instead of a toothbrush. Inevitably, tooth decay was much more common and I saw some frightful dental sights, not only in the Lane or similar poor roads. At five or six you are not really aware of other people's teeth, but on the very first day I started at Staples Road there was one lad from Englands Lane with a major dental problem. He didn't seem to be in pain, but all his front teeth were already rotten and most of the rest were rapidly going the same way. After some months he didn't turn up at school and as he never reappeared I assumed his family had moved elsewhere.

At the other end of the age spectrum, my grandmother was one who, for the reasons described, gradually became almost toothless, although she still managed quite well without them. In fact, she never lost all her teeth as, right to the end, one upper front incisor remained in place and although she used to say 'When that one goes, I go', it was she who went first.

Against this background it was hardly surprising that when the NHS finally began in July 1948, aiming to offer cradle to the grave treatment according to need rather than ability to pay, it led to a rush of patients eager for free teeth and glasses. For years my grandparents had been using spectacles given to them, by whom I don't know, but now was the chance to get some made to their own prescription. However old habits and fears died hard and they, unlike many others in the Lane, never joined the queues for a set of dentures. Readers who were around in those days may well remember false teeth soaking in Steradent by the side of the bed.

Who coped with this fresh demand? At that time there weren't many doctors, dentists or opticians in the town although as the years passed their numbers grew substantially. I certainly can't remember them all, so will mention only those I recall from the early NHS years.

The aforementioned Mr Frederick Moser lived and practised at 188 High Road, next to Parrotts the large drapers, almost opposite what is now Mackays, the clothes shop. In 1948–49 I went to him to have two teeth removed under gas to prevent overcrowding and I remember him as a very pleasant man. I don't know when he retired but later I used to go to Mr Derek Wright in High Beech Road, a few doors along from the Loughton Masonic Hall, although some years later he moved his surgery to King's Green, near the War Memorial. Businesslike but friendly, he was always happy to discuss the apparatus and materials he used which helped make a potentially unpleasant experience more tolerable. Mr Wright died about 2003.

Mr John Carter (no relative) practised on the corner of Lower Park Road, but I never went there, and Chris Pond recalls that another Buckhurst Hill County High pupil, David Johnson, a near-contemporary of mine, used a dentist in Algers Road, opposite Algers Close.

The school dentist at the time was located in what is still the Health Clinic in Buckhurst Way, and I won't remind readers of the experience (mentioned in the chapter on schools) of many of the Staples Road pupils unfortunate enough to be sent there. All I would say is that if ever a place led to a lifelong fear of dentists, that was it.

In those days I suppose there were good reasons to be afraid of dentists. Even though Loughton was well-off, their waiting rooms were cheerless places with a smell of mixed antiseptic and anaesthetic that put you on edge as soon as you came through the front door, not helped by knowing that the equipment used in the 40s and 50s was still rather primitive and potentially painful.

As for doctors, my memory of the practice that our family attended is that it provided a wonderful service. The three GPs I remember were Exell, Bell and Walker and at various times we saw them all. It was mainly Dr Exell who attended so frequently when I had scarlet fever in the dreadful 1947 winter – I don't know who paid for that, but assume it would have been my father, although he may have been helped by being on a 'panel' which covered young children. Their practice was at the top of Station Road, No 9, next to the Lopping Hall, and I remember that you would enter and then have to knock on the tiny hatch to the left which the receptionist would slide open. There was never any argument or prevarication about appointments. You simply sat and waited until the hatch opened, your name was called and then it closed again.

My cousin Maureen remembers that, on a visit from Bethnal Green to Loughton, probably in 1947, my mother asked her to pop round to the doctor's in Station Road for the medicine I was to be given for tonsillitis as at that time there was a dispensary on the premises. It was taken on trust that the medicines would be collected by the patients for whom they were intended as sure enough it was, waiting in the box in the lobby. Later, if we needed a prescription, by then free of course, Hutchins was the handiest and most popular chemist, in the same premises it has now occupied for over a century.

Like most others in the Lane we had no telephone so we had to go to the surgery if we felt it necessary to ask for a house call. The request was never refused as in those days it was quite normal to seek one. Most of the time in the late 40s–early 50s, whichever of our doctors called, any treatment I received seemed to consist of keeping the bedroom too warm, the windows closed, drinking copious amounts of lemon barley water and having my chest rubbed with camphorated oil. However, it generally seemed to do the trick.

With apologies for omissions, the only other name I remember from those early post-war years was that of Gerald Kirkland (the husband of Josie Collins, mentioned elsewhere), opposite Grange Court.

Even though charges to cover at least part of the cost of prescriptions, teeth and specs were introduced only a few years after the NHS started, one of the best things about the changes was that there was no need to rely, as my grandparents frequently did, on quack cure-all remedies that even in the late 40s were sometimes sold by door-to-door salesmen. Strangely enough, although the 'medicine' may only have been coloured water they swore they felt better for taking it.

Over the next 20 years or so Loughton saw the establishment of other doctors' and dentists' practices and later of larger health centres. One practice from the 60s was that of Dr Louise Mitchell and Dr Paul Kliber on King's Green before they moved to 38 Forest Road – later Dr Mitchell converted a house, 11 Station Road, and the practice grew.

Although diagnosis and treatment may have become increasingly successful and sophisticated since the 40s and 50s it now seems harder in Loughton to build a consistent relationship with one doctor, more difficult to make an appointment, house calls are like gold dust and prescriptions, for those who have to pay, aren't cheap any more.

As far as opticians are concerned, there weren't many to satisfy the new demand. I'm told Riders used to be near the Lincoln Hall but I don't remember it, and for many years the most prominent firm was Bird and Fairley in Brooklyn Parade, which opened for business in 1947. They of course are still flourishing, despite the fact that many competitors, including some who are part of nationwide chains, have now opened in the town. On calling in there I was told that, when they first opened, the shop window looked almost like a funeral parlour with dark curtains protecting the interior from view and only a few pairs of spectacles on display. Apparently this was to ensure that customer sensitivities, particularly those of the ladies, were not upset by members of the public in the street watching them try on different pairs of glasses.

In the times we are considering, Loughton had no hospital within its own boundaries but residents seemed to have much wider access than at present, our only choice now being either Whipps Cross, on the edge of London but with Epping Forest directly opposite, or Princess Alexandra in Harlow. Even though none of those that have gone were actually in Loughton itself, they were still much appreciated by many town residents who joined with others in the district to resist their passing.

One of those was the small Forest Hospital in Roebuck Lane, which opened just before the First World War. It had an excellent reputation and some Staples Road pupils went there to have their tonsils and adenoids removed. Local GPs often looked after their patients when they were admitted and one was Maureen who, in the 60s, was in the Forest for quite a serious operation. She recalls the nursing care as superb, the ward spotless, and with an excellent menu. The hospital had a terrific chef and soon after the operation, when she was able to eat, he came to her bedside personally to ask if there was anything special she fancied. The answer was minced chicken and rice, probably an unusual choice for the time, but he duly produced it for her. When she was discharged I drove her home and she said it had been more like a hotel than a hospital. Despite loud and lengthy protests most parts of Forest Hospital closed in 1984.

The same year saw the demise of Harts Hospital, another of the Forest Group of Hospitals, converted in the 20s from a large old house in Woodford Green and which dealt mainly with serious chest problems. There was something of a local uprising in the form of the 'Save Harts Hospital' campaign but the closure was already a done deal and campaigners' efforts were ignored, just as were those of others who tried to save the Connaught in Walthamstow and the Honey Lane cottage hospital in Waltham Abbey where one of the Old Buckwellians hockey team, Frank Hardy, was sent in the 60s for an emergency operation after breaking his nose in a local accident. Some Old Bucks visited him there and it seemed a very cosy place.

I remember the tiny Jubilee Hospital in Broomhill Walk near the Woodford Green Cricket Club very well as I used to go there for regular checks on a perforated eardrum, a problem from childhood. That was a lovely hospital – a bit old, yes, as it was opened in 1899, having been started on the occasion of Queen Victoria's Diamond Jubilee, but very efficient, with friendly caring staff. Economies of scale dictated that the Jubilee was far too small and in 1985, despite the usual fruitless local resistance, it became yet another casualty of NHS reorganisation.

My father was operated on in St Margaret's Epping, having been admitted via its Accident and Emergency Department, to which most Loughtonians would then be taken and the hospital enjoyed a high reputation through the 40s, 50s and 60s and much later. Nowadays, of course, the ambulance goes to Whipps Cross, but although Whipps was obviously a lot bigger, we always regarded St Margaret's as our main hospital. A few specialist units are still there but its A and E was another facility which many Loughtonians were particularly sad to see closed down, particularly after such a long history – St Margaret's dates back to the mid 1830s when it was the Epping Union Workhouse.

Many Loughton residents went up to London on the train, for example, to the London Hospital, Whitechapel. Others from the town, including my father, were treated in Wanstead Hospital, Hermon Hill, the setting of a late 60s TV comedy series *Doctor in the House* but that is yet another that has gone, the main part closing in 1986, although some units stayed open for a few years more.

As regards animal care, in the post-war years, the first vet I remember was Miss Cradock in Church Hill, near Warriners the funeral directors. Just as there were few doctors and dentists, vets in Loughton were also scarce. In fact she may have been the only one because the two names I could find of people involved in Loughton animal welfare immediately before the Second World War were ones I have never heard of before. These were a vet, Mr J Chapman, who lived (and presumably practised) in the High Road near Traps Hill, and a Miss M M Smith at the bottom of Forest Road, who was intriguingly listed as a canine nurse.

Although I'm sure the charges were reasonable many post-war Loughton animal lovers were unable to afford treatment for their pets. Those who genuinely could not meet vets' bills could turn to the PDSA (People's Dispensary for Sick Animals) and on one day each week their white van would park by the Triangle at the end of Smarts Lane, so that the vet could attend to the queue of anxious owners with their animals. As I remember, there were two who alternated and whether dressing a pet's wound or merely clipping claws they always did what they could, and most problems could be dealt with on the spot. Nobody was asked to pay, but there was a box for owners to make a contribution, however little that might be. As they were so grateful for this service I'm sure everybody managed to donate something, and I believe the norm was half a crown (12½ pence).

As far as I remember our dog Floss and her rabbit-hunting spaniel friend Pat, who belonged to my uncle Harry, rarely needed to visit the vet. However Aunt May from 47 Smarts Lane always had cats and when necessary she would take them to Miss Cradock. Sometimes I would save her the journey and take them for her, and found Miss Cradock always friendly with a genuine love of animals. Later she went into partnership with Miss Hull and the two worked together for some years in Church Hill before moving to premises at the bottom of Station Road. Later on, I think it was when Miss Cradock retired, Miss Hull entered the veterinary practice in Palmerston Road, Buckhurst Hill, owned at the time by Mr Hart, and subsequently taken over by Mr Reid.

That practice, the Palmerston Veterinary Hospital, is the one we have stayed with for many years although in the same way that the number of doctors, dentists and opticians increased in the 50s and 60s, so more vets also established practices either in Loughton itself or nearby, although, as Chris Pond remembers, there was a period from about the mid-80s to 2000 when there was no vet in Loughton until one opened in Roding Road, followed by another in Debden Broadway.

14 What do we miss?

This book is mainly concerned with overall impressions of Loughton in the 50s and 60s but although I remember how most of the town used to look in those days I realised as soon as I started it that, in the limited period of those two decades, so many old buildings fell before the bulldozer that to try to list them probably required a separate volume. Fortunately one such work is available and I therefore commend Chris Pond's key 2003 Loughton and District Historical Society publication, *The Buildings of Loughton and Notable People of the Town*. This provides a wealth of historical facts as well as much absorbing social comment.

I have tried to recall the most flagrant changes to the town's appearance, particularly along the High Road, but there were numerous more minor ones, sometimes involving buildings which many present Loughtonians, especially those under 50, may be unaware even existed.

Loughton's present haphazard aspect is far removed from the relaxed semi-rural one that lasted well into the 50s. After that the town began to suffer badly from too much piecemeal change, crude planning and the destruction of some delightful old houses that were too often replaced with dreadful shop façades. These factors accelerated in the 60s and taken collectively had a notably detrimental effect. However, I believe the most damaging individual changes were those brought about by the demolition of the Crown Hotel, the 'Gardens' opposite the former Post Office (now The Last Post pub) the Century Cinema and Victor's handyman's store.

For almost a century the Crown Hotel's large forecourt had been an assembly point for horse-drawn vehicles then much later for omnibuses – in the First World War, when the buses first served Loughton, the Crown was their terminus. It was also from there that in November 1879 the working-class men from the town, many from Smarts Lane and Forest Road, strode into Epping Forest on their very last lopping expedition.

There used to be guest rooms, but by the 50s there was no longer a demand for them and, even for those who appreciated its historic links, the Crown was simply one of several excellent Loughton pubs. Despite its occasional use for both official and private functions its continued existence depended on its success as a public-house and by the end of the 50s, given that there was such a huge but unproductive area in front, its viability had probably ceased. A few years later the decision was made to maximise revenues from the site, a pattern already spreading inexorably to other parts of the High Road. The ghastly complex that replaced the old Victorian inn, kitted out as mock Tudor just before the War, is described in another chapter, but it still bears repeating that, treated more sympathetically, at least some of the unspoiled character of the south end of the High Road might have been preserved.

No doubt commercial temptation caused the inevitable doom of the 'Gardens', and the creation of the soulless developments along the High Road from what is now Halifax plc northwards to Travelcare, just before Woolworths. Until the end of the 50s the High Road had remained nicely 'villagey' and those gardens were a major component of that impression. Both charming to look at and pleasant to be in, they were too small to be called a park, but big enough to allow us to pass the time of day in plenty of attractive green space. Older residents especially enjoyed watching the world go by, relaxing on a shady bench or even simply standing out of the rain under one of the large trees, and there was often somebody there for them to chat to.

One hot morning, probably in 1950, my mother came home rather excited. The well-known actor Jack Watling, then a Loughtonian, lived for a time in Alderton Hall, off Alderton Hill and she had spoken to him in the Gardens. She did tell my father and me what he said but all I can remember is that he made a good impression. Apart from scores of films and TV shows, Jack had another claim to fame, as it was he who crowned the 1949 Loughton Carnival Queen.

Loughton lost those gardens in the early 60s, finally making way for the construction of the London Co-operative Society supermarket, at the time the second largest in the country, and also described elsewhere in this book. It traded for 20 years with limited success, eventually being converted into six separate shops, Centric Parade. It would have been so much more rewarding if a way could have been found to preserve the Gardens and to retain their charm while still allowing harmonious development elsewhere in the High Road. How pleasant that part of Loughton would look now, but once the LCS bought the site, there was no hope of that happening. Chris Pond suspects that the LCS owned the site, undeveloped, for a good 10 years before its big new supermarket opened in 1962.

Before the War the Loughton Cinema, later the Century, was owned by Conrad March and he probably did very well from it in the days when film-going was hugely popular. The Century Cinema's ignominious 1963 closure after 35 years is also described elsewhere but it is another classic example, perhaps not as notorious or large-scale as the first two, of the sort of damage that was allowed to happen by Loughton's planning laws of the 60s. (In fairness, planners could only work to the law as it existed and none of the demolished old buildings were protected – as most Victorian buildings still are not.)

The Century building, although attractive in an ugly way, had to go as it was outdated and suitable only as a cinema. Like other High Road buildings demolished in the 50s and 60s, some of them grand houses over 100 years old, perhaps its useful time was long gone, but it is hard to imagine anything drearier than its replacement.

The dire impact of Victor's destruction on the south end of town is still clearly visible from the High Road even though the former quaintly spired bakery actually stood about sixty yards away to the left, on the fork of High Beech Road and Smarts Lane. Its demolition to make way for a poky little car park finally took place in about 1970, a clear sign that Loughton, already much changed, was going to see more developments like those of the 60s.

Before finally being sold to the Essex County Council I don't know who owned St Margaret's, the very large old house that in the mid-50s was used as St Margaret's Children's Home. It used to occupy the site that became the Homecherry House retirement complex, next door to the Loughton Union Church and, thanks to Chris Pond, I now understand that it was one of the buildings James Cubitt, a long-term Loughtonian, designed for the Union Church pastor, Vivian. I often visited one of my Buckhurst Hill County High friends, Victor Kirton, who lived there with his brother, Andrew, and about 20 other children of both sexes. The two biggest of the numerous bedrooms served as dormitories and downstairs there was a vast dining room, an equally big playroom plus offices and living quarters for Dick and Margaret Robinson, who ran the home for some years in the 50s. The rear grounds were relatively modest but as the house was set back 70 yards or more from the High Road the terraced front garden was large enough for a grass tennis court on the lower level, with a great deal more room besides, although when I visited there it was mainly being used for football, cricket and rounders.

My visits lasted until Victor left both Buckhurst Hill County High and St Margaret's in 1954, and in that period I made other friends among the residents. Some, like Victor, were there for a long time, others suddenly appeared then equally quickly disappeared but all of them, especially those who seemed very withdrawn, were well cared for by the Robinsons, with whom I talked quite often. I don't remember many visitors there as the authorities seemed to discourage them, so perhaps Dick and Margaret bent the rules a bit in my case. Dick didn't mince his words and would often complain to his paymasters about limited funds and, at roughly the time Victor left, I believe the Robinsons also moved on. St Margaret's, despite the underprivileged background of some of the children, was a cheerful place but I imagine most Loughton residents took little notice as it was protected from view by thick high hedges along the front and sides.

I don't remember how long before the final destruction of the old house St Margaret's had ceased to be a children's home, but it probably came down in about 1984. It was still in existence in about 1972 when Sandra and I called in to pass on some toys our two boys no longer used. Although its end was outside the period we are looking at, my memories of the home are very much centred on the 50s and I can still remember Victor, his brother, Andrew, and others from 50 years ago including (if names are permitted here) Brian Sanderson, Barry McAuliffe and Iris Murphy, but I have no idea where any of them are now.

I also have a memory of a place where it was not the building itself that altered, but more the local perception of it when its purpose was changed. In the 50s attitudes to mothers of children born outside marriage were often unsympathetic. St Faith's in Station Road was a classic example of old-fashioned Loughtonian thinking, and of how many of the young mothers facing that problem were stigmatised. It used to provoke much comment of the 'nudge nudge, wink wink' sort, plus a fair amount of the 'nimby' kind. Sometimes when I passed St Faith's (which had originally been a large private house) on my way to the Central Line and the City, I wondered why on earth the sign outside had to proclaim 'St Faith's Home for Unmarried Mothers' indeed why there had to be a sign at all as it seemed an unnecessary throwback to a time when Loughton society was much more clearly stratified. When the home closed, the name disappeared and the property was later extended. It is now a residential care home for the elderly.

An earlier example of a large old house whose time had passed being pulled down was Newnham House right on the edge of town, replaced by many flats in 1962. On a smaller scale, Willow Cottage, a delightful weatherboarded building almost opposite Oaklands School, was well over 300 years old when it was destroyed and replaced in the 60s by The Willows, a block of flats as unimaginative as any in Loughton.

With prime building land becoming ever more valuable it was understandable that in the 60s and later decades it would be impossible, given the high staff and maintenance costs, to resist the temptation to sell other large properties like Nafferton Lodge or Algers House at the south end of town, and for developers to flatten them and squeeze as many new houses or flats as they could onto the site.

It wasn't only the town centre that suffered. There are still some picturesque houses in the first part of Lower Road, the old northern route into Loughton, but further down the road and then into Church Hill many quaint old dwellings have been demolished creating a mix of shops, public offices and commercial premises almost as chaotic as anywhere in the High Road itself.

One sudden but understandable change badly affected the bottom end of Traps Hill, alongside Loughton Cricket Club. When playing for Loughton, which I did in the 50s and 60s, players and spectators alike admired the row of huge elm trees on the south side of the ground. A lofted straight drive to clear them was a very big hit but it could be done – some older spectators may remember Gordon Spooner from the 50s who made a habit of peppering those elms. It was tragic when, following one of the 60s outbreaks of Dutch Elm disease, they all had to come down since they were the ground's most impressive feature. Even without the elms, Loughton's cricket field is still among the most attractive in Essex, but when the trees were first removed the shock was awful and for years the lower part of Traps Hill looked even more naked than it does now. Perhaps one consolation was that nobody could blame it on the planners or property developers.

Anybody interested in these topics might care to know that various 'before and after' photographs exist showing how the razing and rebuilding of Loughton's most significant sites, and of various smaller ones, dramatically altered the town's appearance. Some such photos can be found in the local history section of the library in Traps Hill.

15 Carnivals, fêtes and fireworks

Many Loughtonians joined in the nation's festivities for the 1977 Silver Jubilee, the 50th anniversary of VE Day in 1995, and the 2002 Golden Jubilee, mainly by holding street parties, but not since the 60s has there been anything matching up to Loughton Carnival Week.

This was restarted under the combined sponsorship of Loughton British Legion and Loughton Community Association, with all proceeds divided between those two worthy organisations. From its post-war revival in 1948 into the early 60s, Carnival Week was held in July and I remember the great sense of anticipation as opening day grew closer, especially if you were lucky enough to be in the procession. Carnival Week seemed to involve most people in the town as well as attracting many from surrounding districts. The people of Debden also decided that they liked having a good time so the Debden Horticultural Society and the Debden Community Association conceived the idea of their own annual week of celebration and as a result the Debden Fair was first held in August 1954 and continued into the 60s.

Both events lasted eight days, the Loughton week beginning at 2 p.m. on a Saturday with an opening ceremony and a very full programme of shows, as well as the first stage of the election of the Carnival Queen and her two princesses. The Loughton fairground was the LNER Sports Ground behind Loughton Station (later the Old Bancroftians' field) and Robert Keeble's Giant Fair, apart from on Sunday, would be open throughout the whole week to the second Saturday. Among the numerous attractions on the weekdays was the Carnival Queen final on the Monday evening but the highlight, at least as far as I was concerned, was the procession on the second Saturday that, from moving off, took over an hour to reach the field, after which Carnival Day itself would be declared officially open. I used to enjoy the procession even more than Brocks' magnificent Grand Fireworks Display, as it was advertised, that literally finished the week with a bang.

The Debden fairground was behind Loughton Hall, with access from Borders Lane, leading on to what is now part of the Epping Forest College site. Debden's programme was not quite as wide-ranging as Loughton's and although the fair, again Robert Keeble's, stayed open throughout the week there were fewer extra attractions. The final Saturday's entertainment, apart from the Carnival procession, was also less varied but I hasten to say that is in no way a critical comment. I am sure readers will understand if in this book I give more emphasis to my recollections of Loughton's own Carnival, which I do recall very vividly.

Loughton Carnival Week was always advertised well in advance in the local papers, by the sale of thousands of programmes and also by stretching a huge banner across the High Road where the town's rather undersized Christmas 2004 decoration was displayed, that is, at the junction with the Drive, across from what is now Cook (formerly World of Pianos) to Haarts, the estate agents. I also seem to remember a similar banner at the other end of town, stretching from the former Royal Standard, now Minx, yet another new restaurant, to the other side.

One year, probably 1949, I was on a combined Cubs and Scouts float with others from the 41st Epping Forest, based at the Union Church, along with boys from St Mary's and St John's. Another time I was one of the Lanites on the flat-backed lorry provided by J Cole & Sons, haulage contractors, and decorated by Smarts Lane residents in Cole's big yard, now yet another a new housing development built between the Carpenters Arms and the Victoria Tavern. Our splendid float was then driven up the Lane (Smarts Lane was still, until 1960, a two-way road) to the assembly point at the Forest Road/Staples Road junction, but although we thought it looked wonderful, we didn't win a prize. Prizes were mostly a matter of honour as for most categories the first was only £2, with £1 for second and 10s. for third.

Without doubt the most impressive and meaningful of all the Loughton Carnivals was the one that was part of the Festival of Britain and Loughton Fair of 1951. In that year Carnival Week was from 21 July to 28 July, but other celebratory events, plays, concerts, dances, fêtes and inter-denominational church services, including a very big one on Loughton Cricket Club's ground, were held as early as 8 July. Another successful event was the Garden Fête in St Mary's Vicarage, approached through gates in Priory Road, and this was repeated a few times in later years.

There were procession entries for tradesmen and firms within Chigwell Urban District and separate ones for outside firms. Many were really outstanding, including floats from the gas, electricity and water boards, various breweries, such as Mann's, Charringtons, Trumans, then still independent companies, local garages and many, many others. Altogether, there were 17 categories and some were obviously specially prepared professional floats that did the rounds of carnivals in the County; most of the other classes, including decorated prams, bikes and cars, horses, plus ladies, gents and children's fancy dress, were 'home-made' but no less splendid for that.

Ron Darvell, who moved in 1948 to Barfields, one of the earliest Debden roads, kindly showed me his copy of the 1951 Loughton programme, as well as his 1956 Debden Fair programme. Ron remembers the Loughton procession route as being jam-packed with cheering, applauding onlookers, and that is how I remember it. He was a competitor for some years in the Debden procession, driving an old but prizewinning ex-London taxi into the 60s, and their route was also flanked by enthusiastic crowds.

After assembling at the top of Forest Road, Loughton's procession would move off at 2.30, following the route along Staples Road, down York Hill, through the High Road, into Station Road, then the lower part of Alderton Hill, along Roding Road, then part of Valley Hill before the final turn into Kenilworth Gardens and the fairground itself. For the benefit of readers interested in the Debden carnival procession, this would assemble at Wellfields, then move along Pyrles Lane, Burney Drive, Etheridge Road, Rookwood Avenue, The Broadway, Chigwell Lane, Colson Road, Homecroft Gardens to finish in the Borders Lane entrance to the Loughton Hall field.

Loughton's event was organised in the name of the Loughton Wards of the Chigwell Urban District Council and the list of officers, committee members, judges, and organisers includes many of the great and good of Loughton and nearby districts, including historians, notable tradesmen, professional men, local officers and most interestingly, to me anyway, Miss José Collins, the internationally renowned music hall star, who made the old hit song *Ta-ra-ra-boom-de-ay* into a national favourite. Miss Collins, who died in 1958, was also one of the carnival procession judges, as was Walter Spradbery, a prominent local artist, who was the mentor and role model for Arnold Smethurst, our brilliant art master at Buckhurst Hill County High throughout all the 50s and 60s. One of the Vice-Presidents, Frank S Foster later, by then Sir Frank, was also President of the Debden Fair.

The Loughton fairground would be teeming, so searching for the mysterious 'Lord Loughton', shown in the Carnival programme as a shadowy pipe-smoking figure was not easy. If you managed to track him down in the fairground, the reward for your efforts, provided you had a programme and were one of the first 10 challengers, was a 10s. prize. He eluded me.

It was always a big fair, indeed, as Mr Keeble labelled it, a Giant Fair, and whatever attraction readers care to think of, I am certain it was there. I was foolish enough to try the chairoplanes, where the centrifugal force of fast whirling chairs on chains would lift you so that you were hurtling round at great speed parallel to the ground. Never again.

Most of the exhibitions and shows were on the fairground site and although there may have been some year-to-year differences, the list included such regulars as dog, cat, rabbit, caged bird, flower and vegetable shows, a baby show, a Motor-Cycle Gymkhana by the West Essex Motor-Cycle Club (in later years I believe this event was staged by the Metropolitan Police), a demonstration by The Women's League of Health and Beauty (which involved synchronised gymnastics holding beach balls), marching bands and cycle proficiency tests organised by Chigwell Road Safety Council. I remember the Staples Road School Dancing Display on the final day of the 1951 fair but that was most certainly as a spectator, not a member of the team.

Many Loughtonians will remember or have been customers of some of the advertisers in that 1951 programme: Reginald Lancashire, 'The Home of Carpets for the Home'; Raymond Leonards, 'Complete House Furnishers'; the Co-op; Loughton House Stores in Forest Road; A J Harrison; Cramphorns; Warnes Outfitters; Thos M Cox, the butcher, or as they called themselves, the Meat, Poultry and Game Contractor; Charles S Foster & Sons, then the town's biggest builders; Patmore Brothers, the garage near the Crown public-house. Most of these ceased trading in the 50s and 60s.

There were four major pavilions on the 1951 fairground, the Community Pavilion set up by the Loughton Community Association, the Legion Pavilion, Pavilion of Arts, with a major contribution by the Loughton Camera Club and the Pavilion of Youth. I visited them all and although such an array was something of a one-off for the Festival of Britain, these organisations were a feature of other years, although on a smaller scale.

Loughton's young people turned out in force, with exhibitions and demonstrations throughout the whole week staged, among others by the Scouts, Guides, Loughton School Cadets, the Boys' Brigade, the Girls' Life Brigade and the Loughton Youth Centre based at Roding Road Secondary Modern School. There were so many opportunities for youth recreation in those days and there was rarely even a whiff of trouble in the town on a Friday or Saturday night.

I remember the British Legion exhibition of wreath and poppy making by disabled servicemen and, even though I was only 10, I was aware that those men and women had made a special sacrifice and I still had the same impression 44 years later when my wife and I visited the British Legion Poppy Factory at Richmond.

Brock's Grand Fireworks Display was always spectacular and as soon as the roped-off viewing area was opened up, the waiting crowds would scamper inside to secure the best spot. From the opening salvo of rockets to the final deafening blast from the maroon that always ended the display, we were never disappointed.

Our family used to put money aside for the fair, and when it was over we were spent out but happy, even though we complained the coconuts were 'stuck on with glue'. We were even delighted with the cheap painted chalk figurines that most of the stalls gave as prizes, or the sad little goldfish in their plastic bags, most of which would soon perish, but which we generally managed to keep going for a long time.

The whole week seemed to show Loughton at its best and most optimistic, and gave the impression conveyed in some of the early 50s photos that, although not much more than 10 miles from Central London, we lived in what seemed like a country town.

Life in the early 50s was not at all easy for many Loughtonians and some considered the Festival of Britain to be a rather dubious gamble. In his programme remarks the Festival Committee Chairman, Councillor Kenneth Lindy, also a noted local architect, on the subject of the reasons for celebration, managed to catch the mood of both the whole country and Loughton itself in what were still tough times:

' "What then" say the critics "have we to be festive about?"
Surely it is right that we should celebrate our undoubted achievements in many spheres? Surely, above all, we should give thanks for the heroism and sacrifice, much of it unknown and unsung, which carried us through the destruction of war and leaves us still free in our homes – free to grouse and free to laugh. The future may look black . . . but we have time to shy at a coconut and drink a pint before we face the future with a grin and murmur, "What a party!" '

Councillor Lindy got it right, but it was not only in 1951. For all the years from when Carnival Week was resurrected until it finally ended, I thought it was the best thing the town ever did and, as I said earlier, there has been nothing to touch it since.

Throughout the 50s, before fading somewhat in the 60s, exhibitions were put on in Loughton, often in the Lopping Hall by among others, camera clubs and horticultural and caged bird societies. The Lopping Hall was used to stage productions by the Loughton Amateur Dramatic Society, Loughton Operatic Society, or rep by the West Essex Repertory Company, as well as occasional concerts and recitals by well-known performers, and sometimes by schools, my own, Staples Road, being one of them. Of course, Lopping Hall is still used for at least some of these activities.

My impression of those days is that there always seemed to be something going on, maybe a garden fête organised by one of the churches, or at The Shrubberies in the High Road (now long gone, the site having become Centric Parade) perhaps a simple jumble sale. As money was still tight for many, these were hugely popular in the 50s and I remember long queues building up outside St Mary's Church Hall followed by a mad rush as the doors opened with, sad to say, sometimes a number of angry squabbles over a real bargain, or if the dealers had come in too early and tried to raid the stalls before their allotted time.

Apart from the Grand Display in Carnival Week, fireworks were an important annual feature from the mid-40s to the late 50s, especially, in earlier years, for residents of Smarts Lane, Forest Road and High Beech Road. The 5th of November was a very big thing for us, and the ingenuity and effort that went into some of the magnificent guys that were wheeled around the town were generously appreciated, even when budgets were stretched.

In the late 40s, into the 50s there were few rules about buying or selling fireworks. You had to be 13 to buy them but, even if the retailer was fussed, it was easy to find a friend or relative to purchase them for you, so it was simple enough to buy bangers made by Brock's, Wells' or Standard, which we would often let off in Epping Forest, well before the big day. Some of these, even the little 'penny bangers' were so powerful that the authorities soon restricted the amount of explosive they could contain but, apart from that, danger ruled the day. Many shops would do very well by selling loose or boxed fireworks, and trade in most of Loughton's newsagents, confectioners and electrical shops, Woolworths as well, was given a useful boost by the memory of Guido Fawkes.

At the corner of Nursery Road and Smarts Lane there is a clearing, which we called The Green, bordered on two sides by those roads and on the others by bushes and trees. There was more grass in the 40s and 50s than now, so it seemed larger then. Continuing an old Smarts Lane tradition, for some years that was where the best 'non-organised' fireworks display I can remember was held, and for that we had to thank Mr and Mrs Howes, the Loughton greengrocers, who lived in High Beech Road with their sons, Bobby and Terry. They would provide a huge chest of fireworks and, to be fair, they made sure that these were treated with respect and only handed out to responsible people to be let off.

The bonfire, which I am sure was easily the biggest in the district, would be piled up in the week before Guy Fawkes night and it was huge, maybe 20 feet high, and I well remember my father climbing up Eatons' longest ladders to load wood and other materials ever higher. It would be topped just before the fire was lit by most of the guys made in the previous few months, although some were craftily kept back and were used more than once. Although many of us would go home afterwards for our own back-garden displays, others would bring their fireworks along, so sometimes there were a few unfortunate surprises. The one I remember best was when a rocket that had been placed in a bottle in the middle of Nursery Road toppled over at the very moment it ignited. That rocket screamed about 80 yards along the road straight towards a row of small cottages at the top of Smarts Lane, rising no more than a few feet along the way before thudding violently into the front door of what I recently confirmed as being No 199. The owner was probably on the Green anyway, as nobody came to the door, and no real harm had been done as it missed the glass.

Building the fire was very much a combined effort. So when, in what I believe was the final year, we held the celebration on the Green, some mean-minded individual deliberately lit the bonfire a few days before the 5th, we all, after the first shock, simply set to and built another one, which in about two days was even bigger and better than before. The downside was that the Corporation of London, which had hitherto given permission to hold our displays on the site, decided that they would have to cease which, although sad, was perhaps inevitable.

After I had completed this chapter Chris Pond discovered an article in *The Times* of 1 November 1957, which states that the Forest keepers had been instructed by Alfred Qvist, then in charge, to set light to the Smarts Lane bonfire:It reads:

'. . . The Epping Forest superintendent said yesterday that instructions were given for a forest keeper to put a match to a 15ft. bonfire [nearer 20 I'm sure] which had taken a month to build on forest land at the top of Smarts Lane, Loughton, Essex. He was not satisfied with control of the fire and débris clearing last year, he said.

A protest has been sent to the Lord Mayor of London by a member of the Chigwell Council seeking an assurance that this is not the end of a centuries-old tradition.'

As stated above, we rebuilt it in two days and had our celebration, but although Qvist's complaint about clearing up was nonsense, the councillor's plea was to no avail, and the Smarts Lane bonfire was never lit again.

As with Loughton Carnival Week, I cannot remember anything to equal those Guy Fawkes nights on the Green, and I hope any readers who remember something of both events will agree with me, and that current Loughtonians who were not there can appreciate how wonderful they were.

16 Memories of Loughton's pubs

I remember Loughton's pubs as such an integral part of 50s and 60s life in the town that I believe they deserve their own separate chapter. Mostly dating from Victorian times, many of them were already very old by the 50s – for example, the Holly Bush and Royal Standard, which were the station pubs when the first station was on the site of Lopping Hall, were both built in the 1850s. In fact, the only one I recall in the 50s and 60s as being reasonably modern, apart from those erected on the new Debden estate, was the Mother Hubbard in Loughton Way where, after home matches, the Old Buckwellians' cricket team plus wives or girl-friends would frequently spend most of the evening with our opposition. As mentioned, it has now made way for new flats.

With a few notable exceptions nearly all of them still survive but some with major differences compared to 50 or 60 years ago. Pubs then were where you went to drink, not eat. As already pointed out there were separate saloon and public bars, and the two sets of customers invariably kept or were kept apart, although saloon bar customers would sometimes go into the public bar for a game of darts. By then the public bars weren't the proverbial spit and sawdust of old, but the furnishings were still frequently very basic – in the Holly Bush, for example, there were simple wooden shelf-like benches fixed to the wall and unpadded high wooden bar-stools. There was normally no music, indeed public bars often had a sign along the lines of 'No singing or dancing allowed – by order of the management', and until the late 50s, no television.

In the 40s and early 50s 'popping down to the local' simply meant just that. Although most of the pubs had reasonable car parks, because there were few cars in Loughton the nearest pub you could reach on foot tended to become your local. If you lived in the lower part of Smarts Lane, the Holly Bush and Royal Standard were handy; for those in the middle it was usually the Carpenters' Arms and at the forest end the Victoria Tavern or the Royal Oak. The notable exception was the Robin Hood on Epping New Road which depended a lot on passing trade from customers in cars or on motor-bikes and bicycles.

From the late 50s, when car ownership became more widespread, the pattern changed; certainly in the Holly Bush, where I then was a part-time barman, the car park was invariably full. This was pre-1967, when there was no drink-drive limit, or roadside breath testing and, although by then various publicity campaigns had made many customers more careful, it was still quite common to try to persuade somebody to have 'one for the road' and I often saw George Smith, the publican, having a quiet word with one or two regulars whose cars were parked outside, suggesting that they might have had enough.

Well before I was officially old enough to be allowed inside a pub I was familiar with the Carpenters' Arms, which is only 50 yards or so from 73 Smarts Lane. From the age of five or six I would often be sent to the off-licence for lemonade, sweets or crisps and, later, when I was with the lads from the Lane on our return from regular football or cricket matches on the Stubbles, we would queue there for soft drinks and a coconut square. Some of the boys would ask for cigarettes but the Martins, who were then the publicans, always refused.

The Carpenters' car park was the assembly point for most of the coach trips jointly organised by Smarts Lane and Forest Road residents to South-end, Canvey Island, Clacton or Walton-on-the-Naze and it was also there, summer and winter, that we played most of our street games. In those days there was a wicket-gate at the back of the car park giving a quick way through from the Lane to Forest Road. The gate is gone but you can still pass through an empty door frame. Through the gate on the left was the entrance to a small factory, now demolished, then used for making plastic components, for what purpose I have no idea but there were often boxes of

81

strangely-shaped black and brown rejects outside. During the War it had been used by Ever-Ready for making batteries and before the factory girls left some very lively celebration parties were held there. I believe that factory was used in pre-war days for making paper bags and was called The Transparent Bag Company.

In the 50s I spent a lot of time in the Holly Bush, and I suppose it is the Loughton pub I remember best. Sometimes, to the annoyance of Mrs Warren who lived in Smarts Lane but whose back garden was alongside the Holly Bush car park, Alan Smith and I would play cricket there, using a tennis ball. We tried to keep the ball down but, to be fair, if it went over her high fence, she would always throw it back. Between the Holly Bush and what was formerly Johnson's the newsagents there used to a very handy passage-way to the car park and to Smarts Lane. The saloon bar entrance was to the left along the passage, the public bar being reached from the High Road. The old stables in the car park was where the two pub dogs, Lassie, a German Shepherd, and Rusty, a Heinz 57 named after his colour, used to sleep. They seemed quite happy in the company of the many pigeons that were also kept there. Rusty would follow anywhere and I often took him into the forest, invariably off the lead, but I'm afraid Lassie, much harder to handle, was often left behind.

When I started part-time work in the Holly Bush, Doris Smith first tested me out in the public bar as I already knew many of the customers pretty well. The atmosphere was friendly, the regulars very sociable and they always enjoyed their darts, dominoes, cribbage and shove-halfpenny. There were normally dogs in the bar, and Doris Smith used to keep a large jar of thick arrowroot biscuits solely for them – they weren't free though, but cost a penny each. In the late 50s a few very intense local communists sometimes used the public bar bringing the *Daily Worker* in with them and after a few pints occasional heated political arguments would start. Today might be different but in those days such exchanges never turned really nasty and George normally cooled things down quickly.

I was soon serving mainly saloon bar customers as many of them were local sportsmen I knew well, but wealthy older Loughtonians also used the Holly Bush and I remember one large evening party of more than a dozen customers who were celebrating a birthday or some other anniversary. Doris or George would normally handle such a group, but both were busy serving other customers, so I handled the round. They ordered a long and very varied list of beer, spirits and liqueurs and after adding the whole thing up in my head and safely putting the money in the big old cash register, I was highly relieved when I finished serving them, but at the end Mrs Smith asked me what exactly each individual drink had cost and how much it all came to. I told her, she checked the prices, wrote them down and added them up herself before, to her delight and my relief, coming to exactly the same answer as me. After that I never looked back.

Although some of the wealthier customers were a bit old-fashioned when it came to accepting that Loughton society was changing rapidly and that social classes were mixing much more freely, the Holly Bush saloon bar clientele was generally very pleasant. One exception I remember most clearly was when serving a customer who was not a Loughton resident, but a reasonably well-known actor who had appeared in various West End musicals and on television. He had probably been drinking too much, as for some reason he started waving his arms about, boasting very loudly about how very much more talented he was than Max Bygraves, and how Max didn't deserve his success. He became even more agitated and by then the whole bar was listening. His outburst continued until George managed to persuade his companion to take him home. That was the only time I saw a saloon bar customer being asked to leave, and even that was only indirectly. We know all about Max Bygraves, but my customer's main claim to fame was starring some years later in fish finger advertisements.

George was a Scot and in those days there was probably no better place in Loughton than the Holly Bush to celebrate New Year's Eve, especially if you liked haggis and good old-fashioned Jimmy Shand and his Band. Excellent Christmas decorations in both bars added to the festive mood and after the final stroke of midnight it was an emotional moment when saloon and public bar regulars joined in shouting New Year greetings across to each other, before combining to sing *Auld Lang Syne*.

Happily it has survived and the Holly Bush remains one of the more relaxing pubs in town, still selling beer from McMullens, one of the few independents of any consequence left. Nowadays, thanks largely to successive Chancellors, a pint of AK is nearly £3 – back in the 50s I'm guessing it was about 1s. to 1s. 3d. (5 to 7 pence). The old skittle alley at the back went sometime before 1949, when I first knew the Smiths, and in 1975 the whole place had an extensive makeover and was also extended. The old alleyway is closed now and, as in other Loughton pubs, the division between the saloon and public bars has been pulled down.

Many Lanites also used the Royal Standard, not only as the publicans, the Knights, made it very friendly but also because many of them, including most of my relatives, were members of the Christmas club. Every week throughout the year they and others, normally from the poorer streets, would go into the public bar and hand over whatever they could afford, in many cases only a few shillings, in exchange for club shares. The organiser seated at a table in the corner would then make a careful entry of every payment in his ledger. The subscriptions were banked in one account and just before Christmas the shares, enhanced by a little interest, were paid out. Mary, my grandmother, was one of many who had never been in a bank in their lives, and the club, apart from the jar of coins for the gas, was the only way they could ever put money aside. For her and many others payout night was always full of anticipation, and even though it may have been only £20 or so, in the late 40s and early 50s that money went a very long way to paying for Christmas. Many wives would go along to see their husbands collect it, making sure they weren't tempted to go mad and undo all the year's good work by spending it over the bar. In those days there were occasional news reports of organisers running off with the precious club money and it is easy to imagine what a terrible blow that must have been but, although pubs in other parts of Loughton probably ran similar clubs, I never heard of any such trouble in any of them. The Royal Standard is no longer a pub and after a century and a half the name has finally passed into Loughton's history. At least the building survives. It now houses Minx, a trendy bar/restaurant.

The early 20th century King's Head is another former pub now bearing an exotic name. After being renamed the Fox a few years ago, it is now an Italian restaurant, Zizzi. Although one would think that its prominent location opposite the War Memorial on Kings Green would guarantee a healthy business, I don't remember the King's Head ever doing particularly well, and it certainly struggled badly at times in the 80s and 90s. I'm told it was much more successful in earlier years but I always felt it was too big and rather lifeless. No doubt there will be readers who disagree about that, but in my day, when playing for or against Loughton Cricket Club, we would often, after vacating the old club-room, by-pass the King's Head and go straight to the Wheatsheaf in York Hill. Rather a pity in a way, as one of the earlier King's Head landlords, Mr Garrett, had been an Essex player and had long and close connections with Loughton Cricket Club.

The Wheatsheaf, built within a few years of the King's Head, was much cosier and the publicans (the Frasers I believe), always created an excellent atmosphere. It had (and still has) the great advantage of an excellent beer garden opposite, which was a wonderful place to wind down on a warm summer evening after a long game of cricket. These two pubs as well as the delightful Kings Green Cottages, were designed by Horace White, a prominent Loughton architect, whose name lives on through the existing practice of White and Mileson, who later drew up the plans for the extension my parents added to 73 Smarts Lane.

Sometimes we would wander further up the hill to the Gardeners' Arms, a pub we now regularly visit for lunch. The cottages next door are 400 or so years old, with others also of great age across the small green opposite, and although there has been some redevelopment in the vicinity the one-time tea-room still looks much as it did in the 50s and 60s. The Gardeners always seems quiet and restful, but there used to be some lively functions and receptions in its intimate small hall. Later, that fell into disuse and the pub needed extensive modernising, but fortunately this was done in the mid-80s without apparent adverse effects to its traditional appearance. Thankfully the amazing view from the small garden is now untroubled but during the blitz in the Second World War Loughtonians watched in sympathy from that spot as parts of heavily bombed London burned 10 or more miles away.

The Foresters' Arms, now about 140 years old, is yet another long-standing pub that has stayed remarkably unchanged, but despite its superb location high in Baldwins Hill with what must be among the very best views of Epping Forest, my acquaintance with it has been relatively limited. Whenever we did go there it was always rather empty but it was obviously doing well enough, as not only has it survived, it has also managed to avoid resorting to a change of name.

One of the Loughton cricketers of the late 60s, Bruce Vandrau, a South African then living in the UK for a year or two, used to have lodgings in the Plume of Feathers, opposite what is now Homebase, so we had a reason to go there a few times after matches. The current building, now much modified, was built in 1859, but the original building on the corner of Englands Lane and Lower Road, is still there. I had never been inside the Feathers before but it was not a particularly enjoyable experience as at that time it was somewhat run down. Because of the behaviour of some customers its reputation had slipped and I remember it in those days as the poor relation among Loughton's pubs. Now the pendulum has swung the other way, and as it always seems busy and the car park invariably packed, the present owners must have discovered a winning formula.

Back in the Lane, I have always known the Victoria Tavern and the Royal Oak as occupying their present sites but the original Royal Oak, built in 1860, was actually in Smarts Lane, before being demolished in about 1905 and rebuilt 60 yards or so further back, having also been turned to face Forest Road. The smaller Victoria Tavern appeared on its current site sometime afterwards. I remember these back-to-back pubs thriving in different ways as the Vic, although it had its regulars from the Lane and nearby roads also, particularly in summer, seemed to attract a lot of passing customers with children who would sit outside in the gardens looking at the canaries, parakeets, budgerigars and golden pheasants that together with various small animals were housed in its large aviary. In the mid-50s, when skiffle was popular, two or three local groups, stringed tea-chests, washboards and all, played in those gardens to enthusiastic audiences, and it was always an excellent free show.

The drink-driving laws accelerated the need for pubs at first to offer a reasonable bar menu but later full restaurant facilities, and both the Victoria Tavern and the Royal Oak responded very well and are still deservedly popular eating places.

My grandfather, although mainly teetotal, was a fairly frequent visitor to the Robin Hood, built in 1865 on the crossroads of Epping New Road and the road from Loughton to High Beach, where there is now a roundabout. I would sometimes go with him and his black spaniel to sit on the small mound overlooking the roundabout and the pub, before taking a lemonade or ginger beer into the deep-set, almost sunken, beer-garden at the back. The Robin Hood had a long history as a meeting place for forest visitors, whether on foot, bicycles or in horse-drawn coaches or, later on, cars. The last time I was there a local society for the preservation of birds of prey, as a fund-raising exercise, had a dozen or so owls of all sizes on view in the beer garden. A few years ago part of the pub was converted to a Thai restaurant.

The 1960s demise of the original Crown Hotel, once an imposing old Victorian inn, and one of Loughton's most historic buildings, has been much lamented in this book, but at least it was some minor consolation that its replacement kept the name Crown, although the word Hotel had to go. After that the new one on the end of the big block of offices and shops built on the original site has been variously called the Rat and Carrot, the Old Crown and until 2005 the Long Bar, which seemed rather overblown as the interior had never been at all noted for its length. At the time of writing it is has undergone yet another conversion to a café/bar called Nu.

Loughton is now so full of licensed bars and restaurants that the relative importance of the pubs that remain is less than it was in the 60s. Also, in the last 50 years, the style, character and, to some extent, even their purpose, has changed almost beyond recognition. Most of my Loughtonian friends firmly believe that the majority, particularly on Friday or Saturday evenings, were probably safer, more relaxing places to visit then than now. Compared with the 50s and 60s the modern style of service seems far more casual, sometimes impersonal, and with most Loughton pubs using touch-screen tills, speed seems of the essence and mental arithmetic is no longer called for.

17 Loughton's worst winters

It is fascinating to recall how Loughton coped under extreme pressure and I have unforgettable memories of life in the town in the winters of 1947 and 1962–63. To some readers these may be meaningless dates but both years are notorious for the most vicious British weather in living memory. It seems remarkable that within the short period covered by this book the town experienced the two worst winters of the 20th century; 1947 being the year of by far the heaviest snowfalls and 1962–63 easily that of the longest and deepest cold spell.

Most Loughtonians will remember the 2004–5 chaos in and around the town caused by a meagre few inches of snow but it was a mere fleabite compared to what fell on Loughton in those unforgettable years. How were we affected? Both periods presented major problems which our local authorities handled manfully, but there were also astonishing opportunities to enjoy those parts of Loughton that had been transformed overnight into our very own winter sports resort. Anybody living in the town in those years must have personal recollections not only of how we endured those freakish conditions but also, for some of us at least, how we enjoyed them.

In the fourth week of January 1947 overnight snow began to fall all over the south-east and Loughton woke up to a white blanket several inches thick. It simply kept coming but what we didn't know was that the first blizzard was only the beginning and those arctic conditions would continue for over seven weeks. I can remember going to bed on Friday after watching heavy snow through my window, waking up eight or nine hours later delighted at seeing more of the same, only to become astounded as it carried on into Sunday by which time about a foot had fallen. My cousin Maureen remembers at least two falls like that, maybe deeper, as well as several more of four inches or so plus innumerable lesser ones. From the end of January to the middle of March there were more days when it snowed in Loughton than when nothing fell, and by the time the last flakes had fallen that winter became not only the snowiest since 1814, but also one of the coldest on record.

My father and I went out together immediately after that first blizzard and we soon came across drifts, much taller than Dad, that high winds had piled against the bushes at the top of Smarts Lane and the hedges along Nursery Road. Conditions further out, around High Beach for example, were even worse. Many people there and also some in the higher parts of the town itself were completely cut off by drifts of 10 feet or more and travel was impossible until the ploughs came out.

My father's firm, Eaton Bros, like all the local builders, was very hard-pressed, especially the plumbers, who were soon struggling to keep up with anguished pleas for help with burst or frozen pipes. At that time most houses had lead piping, notoriously prone to bursts, and which had to be worked on with great care by plumbers with blowlamps 'wiping' the joints. My father had previously lagged all our pipes, inside and outside the house, but to be sure he had also wrapped some old jackets and trousers round them and we had very little trouble, although both Maureen and I remember him warming up those in the outside lavatory with hot water bottles rather than take the risk of using his blow-lamp. Like a number of other men from the Lane and Forest Road who worked in the building trade, he did many favours for neighbours, particularly elderly ones with plumbing or in some cases serious draught problems caused by the sub-zero winds. Without that help some of those old people, even inside their cottages, could easily have succumbed to hypothermia. Ironically, in the big thaw that followed the harsh conditions, Eatons had even more to do, as pipes which warmed too rapidly after being frozen developed yet more leaks.

At first all the youngsters in the Lane, some adults too, when they weren't fighting a losing battle trying to clear their pathways, had a great time. Apart from the inevitable giant snowmen, we made a slide that ran diagonally some thirty yards across the Carpenters' Arms car park then lined up to see who could speed fastest and furthest along it. When it was covered by fresh snow, we made it again. We sent many huge snowballs rolling down the long slope of the Stubbles, the big clearing off Nursery Road, and they became ever bigger as they tumbled down the incline.

Helped by us shoving from behind some expanded to well over six feet across, and there they stayed in a long line for nearly two months, finally vanishing in the big thaw.

The Carpenters' Arms was also the scene of almost military style battles between the Laneites and our friendly rivals from Forest Road. Sometimes up to 20 children aged from about six, like me, to 13 or 14, built great piles of snowballs before lining up on either side of the car park to begin hurling them as fast and hard as we could. We staged these mock combats a few times in that winter, but there were never any winners or losers.

When the big freeze was deeply set we played ice hockey on Strawberry Hill Pond, the Gravels as we called it, using improvised sticks made from old fence palings or conveniently shaped tree branches, with big stones for pucks that we sent skimming across the surface with a musical bouncing sound. When we used hammers to break the ice for the water birds it was probably already four or five inches thick. Although we tried to give those and other birds what help we could all through that period we came across many large and small feathered bodies.

Sometimes adults came with us at weekends when we went further afield to the slopes at Drummaids opposite Staples Road School, alongside Warren Hill or, most crowded of all, behind the Warren Wood pub on Epping New Road. A few experienced ones were on skis but most of us made do with home-made sledges like the one Uncle Harry built for me out of wooden offcuts, but with proper metal runners lubricated with motor oil. I remember some very big posh sledges overtaking mine, often with four or five riders holding on to each other, as well as others simply happy to skid down on tin trays.

On the worst days of those seven weeks Staples Road School had to close, not so much because we couldn't get there, but more so because at times the dreadful outside toilets were frozen, but at least it stopped them smelling. I remember that we made many long slides in the playground but amazingly, we were never stopped from doing it.

The novelty began to wear off though and 1947's winter soon became a huge challenge. Although those seven weeks may have been a winter wonderland for Loughton's children and, at first, almost a relief from post-war deprivation for the adults, the severity of the cold and snow was causing great hardship, particularly in more remote parts of the district. After more blizzards, many roads, major and local, had become impassable, trains stopped running and Loughton suffered power cuts. An acute shortage of coal affected the town badly even though we had big coke and coal yards right next to Loughton Station. Like everybody else, we had to switch off all electricity for five hours every day, and so had no light and very little heat. We in 73 Smarts Lane were luckier than some as my father had built up a reasonable store of wood salvaged from building jobs, as did my relatives further down the Lane, but it was not uncommon to see residents from other roads pushing wheelbarrows or prams towards the forest, struggling against the snow to gather whatever branches they could.

In the middle of February, when it snowed nearly every day, I became one of the few people in the Lane, maybe the only one, to be injured as a direct result of the weather. Somebody in one of the snowball fights must have accidentally scraped up a stone with a handful of snow and squeezed it so hard that the ball had a very solid centre. That snowball hit me directly in the left eye and I was immediately rushed round to our doctor's surgery in Station Road where the examination took a long time. The eye was bloodshot and bruised and I couldn't see through the swelling but, after a week indoors my vision had returned to normal although as Dr Exell confirmed, it had seemed much more serious at first.

My troubles weren't yet over. In the second week of March I caught scarlet fever which in those days was a notifiable isolation disease but, as the local hospital was over-stretched with severe winter-type cases, my five-week incarceration was spent at home. Although in all that time Dr Exell called in about three times a week, I was feeling better after only a few days and was able to watch the last of the 1947 snow through my bedroom window. During the great cold spell icicles sometimes at least three feet long had gathered and were hanging from most of the roofs in the Lane and even through the window I could hear their continual dripping as with temperatures climbing a bit they began to melt away. There was also a constant dull thudding from outside as thick melting snow on the Lane's smooth slate roofs gradually slid down before falling to the ground with a massive thump.

In mid-March Loughton had a final spectacular white-out, but immediately after that a very rapid thaw set in which led to further local troubles including a plague of burst pipes and water mains. Maureen remembers better than me how tough it had been for most of us since, as well as having little fuel, there were also food shortages and we sometimes had to get by on even tighter rations. Local farmers had lost livestock but that wasn't all as the thawing snows left fields awash all over the district and led to big floods all along the River Roding which had burst its banks even before being further swollen by the violent rainstorm that finally washed most of the snow away. The floods took many weeks to subside and even after that clearing up took a very long time.

As far as temperatures were concerned 1962–63, the other dramatic winter, was even worse, although the snows never reached the volumes of 1947. Not only was it the coldest of the 20th century but we also endured the lowest temperatures since 1740.

However, again we had extraordinary amounts of snow and I remember when it started. Boxing Day 1962 had been icy cold and overcast all day and at about 9.30 p.m., as I was driving up King's Head Hill, Chingford, having spent the day at Sandra's in Enfield, the snow started. It didn't build up gradually but right from the beginning fell in very large flakes and in the 10 minutes or so from there to the bottom of Smarts Lane where I had a rented garage, about two inches had already accumulated. The next day it snowed hard in bursts and by the end of it nearly a foot had fallen. Some of it was cleared quickly but a lot more fell two days later and most Essex roads became temporarily impassable.

To their credit, whenever snow fell, often before it even started, the local authorities moved very fast with gritters, also deploying ploughs and bulldozers when necessary. Despite such dreadful conditions there seemed to be a great determination on the Council's part to do what had to be done without complaint, buckpassing or excuses about budgets and the lack of resources. Grateful residents like my parents, who knew many council employees, some of whom were from the Lane, often praised the good job they were doing. Although the roads were cleared very efficiently, temperatures were always so low, about 5 centigrade below average for around six weeks, that most of that initial snow stayed frozen on open ground until early March, and whatever fell later settled on top of it.

We had a lot more snow, but it fell less frequently than in 1947 and, unlike in that previous hard winter, there was also a great deal of very dangerous freezing fog. We had some sunny intervals too and sometimes took advantage of those bright spells to go into Epping Forest, which was a massive bonus not, as in 1947 for gathering a little extra fuel, but simply for taking in the unbelievable snowscapes. Walking along Baldwins Hill one weekend I came across an elderly man in a fur hat with flaps that covered his ears who was almost frozen stiff as he tried to paint the remarkable view from the Foresters Arms down towards Baldwins Hill Pond. We talked for a bit but he had to give up and took some photographs instead, with the intention of copying them in oils later. He was one of quite a few hardy artists we came across, and one Sunday morning, after an overnight snowfall, we saw a couple on Kings Green in front of the King's Head, trying to capture a totally white Loughton on canvas while the snow was still fresh on the ground.

It was toboggan heaven again in all the same local places, but this time there were many more people. Although the snow on the sledge and ski runs soon became hard-packed and worn there was normally not long to wait for a fresh fall to restore perfect conditions. 1962–63 was so uniquely cold that the ice on the local ponds and lakes became thicker than ever before and although some national newspapers bemoaned the lack of skaters, I remember Connaught Waters as the charming setting for some very elegant performers.

One Sunday morning, probably about mid-February, I was there with a group of friends enjoying great long slides across the lake and joining other local residents enjoying a good time. Then one of the craziest things I ever saw happened.

Two minis, one green as I recall, the other white, simply drove straight onto the ice. I didn't see them coming, although they must have driven out of the forest, as the ditch around the roadside car park made it impossible for them to make it onto the lake from there. They then drove, or rather, slid around on the lake for several minutes, skidding in and out of the islands, making a lot of people increasingly nervous and angry, so much so that most of them, many with young children, retreated hastily to the safety of the banks. Maybe the drivers had tried their mad stunts elsewhere and knew the ice was safe, as the minis made absolutely no impression on it, but their antics certainly intimidated the locals who were simply having a good time. They finally drove off the ice onto the shallow bank on the far side from Rangers Road, then into the forest, vanishing as suddenly as they arrived. I never knew whether anybody was quick enough to take their numbers but I assume not, as the incident wasn't even mentioned in the local papers.

There was obviously a downside to that winter for all the neighbourhood sportsmen as for months every single local outdoor match was called off. Even when it wasn't snowing, both day and night temperatures mostly stayed below freezing, regularly falling to record lows and underneath the snow-covered pitches the ground was as hard as iron. In those days I was playing hockey for the Old Buckwellians and every fixture from January to the end of March had to be cancelled, first through snow and frost, then by the boggy conditions following the thaw.

One link between the two winters particularly for Laneites, was Jack Street who, as mentioned earlier, owned the dairy a few yards down the road from No 73. Even before 1947 he had delivered our milk for many years but in that harshest of winters and again in 1962–63 he invariably turned out at some point each day, sometimes battling against conditions that would have defeated less determined men. As he told me more than once, he owed it to his loyal customers.

In early March the thaw set in but the aftermath of the big freeze was nothing like as bad as in 1947. True, the Roding spilled over again but the flooding was on a much lesser scale and Loughton life returned to normal very quickly.

There was a lot of snow in other years in the 50s and 60s, much more than we expect now. Our town will probably never again experience winters remotely as harsh as the two I have described but if the weather did become extreme again I would be uncertain how our present local authorities would cope. We can never be sure but as global warming is likely to bring milder conditions from now on, Loughton can probably relax unless, as some experts predict, the Gulf Stream is switched off. If that happened we could well have a '47 or '63 winter every year.

18 Getting around

In the years immediately after the Second World War most Loughtonians didn't own cars so our dependence on public transport was much greater than it is today. However, other residents I have talked to confirm my recollection first as a young child travelling to relatives in the East End then later going to school and to work in the City, that local transport services were excellent.

In the pre-supermarket days of the late 40s and 50s those of us without cars who didn't have their groceries and other essentials delivered either walked to the local shops or, if it was too difficult, caught a bus there and back. It was also not unusual to see ladies from even quite wealthy parts of Loughton riding into town on a bicycle, the old-fashioned sit up and beg kind with a wicker shopping basket in a cradle on the front, which they could leave unchained outside any shop in town without fear of it being stolen.

The majority of present-day residents take the Central Line for granted as only residents of nearly 60 or over have personal experience of the old LNER (London and North Eastern Railway) steam trains that preceded it. Loughton Station, very futuristic when it was completed in the early 40s, replaced the old one that had operated nearby for about 75 years, and was intended to be ready for electrification to Loughton and beyond. Those pre-war plans were obviously delayed by the hostilities but were implemented as soon as possible when they ended. (See the LDHS publication, *The Loughton Railway 150 Years On*, 2006.)

It is easy to sentimentalise over steam trains, but even though some may remember them as noisy, smoky and smelly, blowing soot over your clothes and with doors that, if thrown open carelessly, were highly dangerous I, like many others have to admit to a very soft spot for them. Travelling on those steam trains sometimes used to lead to arguments, especially on a hot day when passengers wanted to open the window for fresh air. People with their backs to the engine would lower the window, which would mean soot annoying those on the other side of the carriage who would insist on closing it. The compromise position of opening it no more than an inch or so didn't do much to lower the temperature, nor did the fact that the discomfort was often increased as smoking was allowed in most carriages just as it was on the upper decks of buses.

My own memories of steam trains are mainly of going with my parents to my mother's sister Marie in Bethnal Green or taking day trips to Southend. It was possible to take a special through excursion train to Southend but I don't recall ever doing that ourselves.

Too much detail can become tedious but it might be useful to outline the example of visits to the East End simply to show how easy it was in those days for Loughton folk to survive without a car. When visiting Marie we had the option of buses or trains and, before the end of 1946, when Bethnal Green Central Line station opened, we would take a steam train from Loughton to Bethnal Green Junction (now simply Bethnal Green) without changing and walk from there. Later, as more stations were electrified, we went only part of the way by steam before changing to the Underground and until 1947 we used to swap from one to the other at Leytonstone until Loughton's turn for the new trains came and the Central Line was extended to the town in November 1948. Going further east, travellers to Epping still had to wait another 10 months before the Central Line was electrified and the now closed Epping to Ongar 'push and pull' shuttle remained steam operated until 1957.

For some years my mother had to do the journey to her sister's pushing me in the big Silver Cross pram bought by my grandparents and it would have been very difficult for her to negotiate the pram up and down station stairs (as my father was still in the army) had it not been for obliging travellers offering to take one end and help. Largely because of such kind folk, my mother preferred the train to the bus until I was able to walk far enough – and, of course, you couldn't take a Silver Cross on a bus. After that she decided that as the stop was nearer to home than the station, the 38A bus was handier.

The 38A, long since discontinued, used to run from Loughton Station to Victoria, a long route which, according to Dennis Coffey, a London Transport bus driver and inspector for over 20 years from 1965, was scheduled to take 1 hour 20minutes but which by the mid-60s when road traffic had greatly increased often took two hours, sometimes nearer three. However, in the 40s and early 50s when we travelled on it from Loughton, or when cousin Maureen and her mother did the journey the other way, it always seemed to run to time. Using the 38A meant a change onto a 653 trolleybus at Kenninghall Road, at the very end of Lea Bridge Road, which would then drop us at the Salmon and Ball pub in Cambridge Heath Road. If you could stand trolleybuses it was a very easy trip, but many people, including a few of my relatives, felt sick from the moment they started to accelerate.

From 1949 to 1951 Uncle Harry and I would go to Spurs' matches by the 38A bus and then change at the Napier Arms, South Woodford, to a 623/625 trolleybus. This was a quadrant terminal loop so the bus could simply run around and it's still there, used for car parking. However, if a trolleybus had broken down, or one wanted to overtake, then it might have been necessary to lower the trolley arms. Sometimes sparks flew and the arms crackled with a noise like an old Frankenstein film and, quite often, particularly if a driver took a corner too fast, they would disconnect from the overhead power lines and fall onto the bus roof with a prolonged series of loud bounces, which meant the bus was stranded. If the conductor, especially in pouring rain, couldn't reconnect them with the long bamboo poles kept under the bus for that purpose we either had to get off and walk or wait for another one.

Older readers probably remember the main routes serving Loughton in the late 40s into the 60s and some of the numbers, for example the 20 and 167, still survive even though the routes themselves may have changed. I'm not sure whether services from Loughton to and from many local and more distant destinations were generally much better than now as, for example, there are more routes into Debden than in the 50s and there are probably nearly as many destinations Loughtonians can reach by public transport as there were then. However, as an example of a lost convenience, the 20 used to run from Leytonstone to Epping, and we sometimes enjoyed the easy 20-minute ride to the Monday Epping market which at that time was vastly more entertaining than the present one. Once you reached Epping it was then simple to catch other buses which ran regularly onward to other parts of Essex and Hertfordshire but getting around that easily without a car has long since been consigned to history. Of course, the hourly H1 runs from Loughton Station to Epping, but takes longer, before going to Harlow.

A welcome change in 1954 was that the 20 Sunday service was extended from the Cock Hotel in Epping so that relatives or friends visiting patients in St Margaret's hospital could catch the bus from Loughton directly to the hospital grounds and in the same year the 20a route was introduced to serve Debden residents. In the late 60s the 20 route was altered appreciably to run from Walthamstow Central station to St Margaret's but from 1968 it was curtailed and went only as far as Debden.

The 167, my old school bus, often used by our family on weekend trips to Southend, ran as now from Debden to Ilford although by a different route, and from there it was easy to catch a train to Southend Victoria. The 254, which had to be a single-decker service so that it could pass under the railway bridge across Roding Road, was introduced as a circular route from Buckhurst Hill to Loughton, then on to Debden and back again to Loughton. This service gave Buckhurst Hill County High boys another useful option when travelling to school and was later extended to South Woodford.

In summer into the early 50s when feeling lazy and not wishing to walk from the Robin Hood to High Beach we sometimes caught the 35A which started at Clapham Common, but this service was suspended in the winter. Now High Beach is no longer served at all, either by this route or the 102, another that ran only on summer weekends. Both these routes came up from Chingford.

In those days there was still both a bus driver and a conductor on board each bus and in the early 50s the conductor carried his or her different coloured tickets in a wooden frame and he would take one out and then clip it in the little machine attached to his front (hence the early term 'clippie' usually applied to a wartime bus conductress). Later the conductors used a more sophisticated machine, the Gibson, which printed tickets in violet ink on a small roll of paper when the conductor wound the tiny handle. I'm reminded by Chris Pond, an authority on local transport history, that the minimum fare on local buses until about 1956 was 2d. (two old pennies) 1d. for a child. Chris has also informed me that, since September 2005, travel for under-16s on routes 20/167/397/549 has been free!

Timekeeping was a matter of great pride and there were inspectors based at the LT garages, including Loughton's, making sure the timetables were adhered to. The inspectors also rode the buses, checking that all passengers had paid for a ticket or in the case of schoolchildren, had valid free passes.

Loughton has had two bus garages. The first, built in the early 20s, remained in use until 1953 after which it has been a Co-op bakery then a DIY store under various different ownerships. The new Loughton Garage across the road operated for thirty years before being closed down in 1986 and later demolished. The new one had been built larger in expectation of rising demand from all the new houses (particularly council properties) being built locally. However it seems it never lived up to expectations. Now buses are kept in the open at the Langston Road Industrial Estate.

If you fancied a little extra comfort and more speed in return for a higher fare there were two handy Green Line routes, the 718 from Epping, later Harlow, to Windsor and the 720 from Bishops Stortford to Aldgate. A few years ago I remember reading an article in the local *Guardian* describing how, with various long waits for necessary but uncoordinated changes, the journey by public road transport from Loughton to Harlow took two hours. How different to 50 years or so earlier! It is better now but nothing like as fast as half a century ago. Green Line stops were infrequent and with relatively little else on the road, in the early 50s the 720 did that journey in only 30 minutes and Bishops Stortford could be reached in 50. If you fancied a day out to Windsor the 718 took you there and we did it once, but only once, as it was a 2¾-hour slog from Loughton through North London and the West End to get there and I remember we thought it really wasn't worth it.

I won't speculate on whether aggression on buses is a consequence of one-man operation both of single or double-deckers, or if it reflects other social changes, but Loughton dwellers in the 50s and 60s had no concerns about 'yob culture' and I remember riding on local buses in the 50s and 60s as being completely risk-free. As there were no crowds of bored or intimidating youngsters hanging around it was also safe to walk home from Loughton Station after working late or spending an evening in town.

In the 50s and 60s pupils from local schools normally behaved very well and certainly didn't throw plastic bottles of tomato ketchup from the top deck of buses onto the road or pavement below, some bursting on passing cars, which is what I witnessed in Loughton High Road, outside the Methodist Church, late one murky afternoon in December 2004. An outraged motorist whose car had been bombed with ketchup stopped the bus but the pupils, most of them still in school uniform, promptly scattered into the darkness and it seems the bus driver told the furious man he proposed to do nothing at all about it and that it was up to him to report it if he wanted to.

Buckhurst Hill County High boys were by no means angels but in the seven years I was there perhaps the worst I heard of anybody from the school doing as far as buses were concerned was for groups of boys to wait for a bus 50 yards or so before a request stop, then to begin running hard as it passed, waving frantically at the driver. When the bus stopped the lads would carry on running straight past and the driver would often see the funny side, but sometimes not, and finally a formal complaint from London Transport was read out in Assembly by Mr Taylor, our headmaster. Unlike present-day local schools Buckhurst Hill County High accepted responsibility, not only for pupils' behaviour in school but in public as well, so he threatened dire consequences for anyone reported doing it again, and that was the end of it.

The 'school run' was unheard of in the Loughton of the 50s and 60s and most of us would get there by bus, train and bicycle or simply walk, unconcerned about feeling unsafe, as local school gates or nearby roads weren't crowded and blocked with cars as they are today. Traffic, particularly in the 50s, was a great deal lighter and cyclists were shown more consideration so unless the weather was bad, from the second year at Buckhurst Hill County High I used to cycle the three miles to school every day. I have to admit, in case I am accused of looking back through rose-tinted glasses, that there was a downside to that. Petty theft from the School bike sheds, and I suppose from other local schools as well, was very common, so most of us would remove our saddlebags and pumps and take the whole lot into school. If left on our bicycles the saddlebags themselves would sometimes disappear and as there was never any security on the school gates there were also a few cases when expensive unchained bikes would go missing.

From the late 40s well into the 50s many children, particularly from Smarts Lane and Forest Road, would ride their bikes up and down the road or play around on scooters and quite a number of these, as well as a lot of our clothes, linen and general housewares, were bought in Club Row, the popular street market near Brick Lane in Shoreditch. Although even better known for its bird and animal market many residents from the less-well-off parts of town would take a bus or train to Club Row for all sorts of new or used bargains and my first three-wheeled bike, a new one, came from there, as did my first two-wheeler, a second hand Phillips. A popular more general market was Petticoat Lane, down Middlesex Street, while Columbia Road in Hackney was favoured for its wide range of plants. However, when I passed the 11 plus my parents bought me a new bike from E G Hatch in the High Road, a Rudge Pathfinder with dropped handlebars and the much-prized 531 lightweight tubing. My father insisting on insuring it which was just as well, as after only a few months it was stolen while I was playing football on Rectory Green, Debden, almost opposite Wellfields, but the insurance claim was upheld and the replacement was the one I rode to school for six years.

Until the Clean Air Act 1956 made the killer London smogs a thing of the past, there were still some really dense fogs which used to come down suddenly, especially near the River Roding. One of these closed in while I was in school, so I had to ride home in it. It may be a cliché but it was hard even to see your hand in front of your face. Foolishly I took my usual short cut across the fields by the Roding and immediately lost my bearings. By the time I found a road again, a five minute journey across the field had turned into 30 minutes of aimless meandering.

In the late 50s some of my friends who wanted a more convenient means of getting around started using motorcycles but they never appealed to me in the slightest and I managed quite happily with public transport, although I did take driving lessons in 1959 in preparation for my first car and the mobility it would bring.

In those days the driving test centre was in Knighton Lane, Buckhurst Hill, and my anticipated ordeal turned into a very unusual affair. The day I took it I was the first candidate on the examiner's list, but he had been delayed by nearly 15 minutes and was extremely anxious to make up for lost time so we drove around and I performed enough of the required manoeuvres to show that I was competent. At that time Queen's Road, Buckhurst Hill, was still two-way and as we went up the hill he told me to drive uphill and stop outside the baker's near the top as he wanted some rolls for his breakfast. I waited outside in the car and when he came back and asked me to move off he said that this would be my hill start. By the time we drove the few hundred yards back to the centre all his lost time had been regained and he told me I had passed. He had taken a bit of a chance but who was I to complain?

At that time, as many residents of Loughton and parts of the district were pretty well off, quite a number of my contemporaries already, with the help of their parents, possessed smart, sometimes new, cars, but a lot of others had to make do with 'old bangers'. There was still a year or so to go before MOT testing came in and some of the wrecks seen on Loughton's streets would never have passed. Three of us from Loughton, a trainee teacher, now a retired headmaster, the second, also at teachers' training college but very soon after sadly killed, plus myself had to use a long leather strap to hold down the bonnet of the teacher's old Morris Minor before setting out for a week in Dorset. That car was later swapped for a Minor convertible, but its roof was so torn that we spent a whole weekend making a new one using a green tarpaulin and thick fisherman's twine.

In the 60s the UK car population doubled and I'm sure that Loughton more than shared in the growth. In 1961 I bought my first car, a used Ford Anglia, 1405 JH, from F G Gates of South Woodford, the cost of £495 partly met by a donation from my parents. My father insisted it should be garaged rather than stand outside the house but like nearly all the houses in Smarts Lane, No 73 had no garage so I had to rent one. Although I was offered one for £1 per week by a lady in Brooklyn Avenue it was not only too far away but also too expensive so I was lucky to hear of another in Smarts Lane itself, a big old shed down a narrow path near the bottom of the road. It had a corrugated roof but it was sound, the doors were strong and it only cost me 12s. 6d.

As was the case with many of my friends from Loughton and the surrounding district, once I had a car I automatically stopped using the town's buses, although until Sandra and I were married I still travelled to the City on the Central Line. Out of interest, while writing this chapter I asked several Loughton friends when was the last time they had used a local bus. In my own case it would be about 40 years ago and the majority of those I spoke to came up with similar answers, although I am pleased to add that Chris Pond, when he read this chapter, was at pains to point out that he had actually travelled on a local bus that very day!

19 Sundays, weddings, funerals and courtship

I read somewhere that children of the 1950s were the last generation when the majority were regular churchgoers but whatever the truth of that assertion it is a fact that church attendances in the last half-century or so have fallen dramatically. I have to admit my own contribution to the numbers has been limited but as this is not the place to give reasons, all I will do is to recall some of my own experiences when I was young and going, like many of my contemporaries at Staples Road School, to Sunday School or to church in the Loughton of nearly 60 years ago. I hasten to say this is not an attempt to refer to every place of worship in town, only those with which I had personal contact.

In the late 40s/early 50s, quite a number of children from Forest Road, Smarts Lane and other parts of town, all aged from about five to eight or nine, went to afternoon Sunday School at 3 o'clock in the Forest Hall, the small mission hall which, much renovated since then, still stands a few yards off the High Road at the bottom of High Beech Road. Although it had its origins in the Plymouth Brethren, in the three years or so I went there I can't recall ever hearing that name mentioned, nor do I recall the words 'evangelical church' which are currently displayed outside.

Sunday School meant spending a whole hour under the eagle eye of Ernie Street, a devout Christian and the yard foreman at Eaton Brothers, where my father worked for well over half his life. Significantly, the Eaton boss at that time was Len Cranwell from Englands Lane, who was very prominent in the life of Forest Hall and who led the Sunday School services. As I used to visit Eatons' yard quite frequently I knew them both reasonably well so it was probably no surprise, especially as for a while my parents were part-time caretakers at the Forest Hall, that my father agreed I should attend their services.

I remember enjoying them at first, but whether that was because of various inducements to attend, I'm not sure. We were given highly-coloured Biblical picture cards, stickers and stamps for attendance and good behaviour. Prizes were handed out at the end of each year and all the children would get something, however small. Every week different children would stand on the steps at the end of the aisle to give readings or sing and often one of them would be given a short baton and he or she would conduct the young congregation, although nobody took much notice of the enthusiastically waved stick. Ernie would watch proceedings very carefully, and if you misbehaved he invariably caught your eye and made sure you knew when he was writing your name down in his little book.

The ultimate threat, but one which I don't remember being carried out, was to be denied going on the Sunday School 'treat', invariably an outing to Clacton or Walton-on-the-Naze, and those trips were always well attended, needing at least three coaches as parents were naturally included.

I have no wish to dismay those who now attend there, but Forest Hall services were occasionally too much for some of the children as a few of the 'fire and brimstone' lay preachers of the time could be rather intimidating, so I was glad that when I joined the 41st Epping Forest Cub pack, based at the Loughton Union Church, I was able to leave. My father agreed that attending church parade each month was enough and as he had, apart from the Forest Hall, rarely set foot inside any other religious building, that seemed very reasonable.

The Loughton Union Church was not a particularly pleasing building to look at (the stark replacement built in the early 70s certainly lacks visual appeal) and the hall underneath in which the Cub meetings were held was sometimes a problem, as it was dark with a low ceiling and numerous supporting columns at intervals across the floor which always interfered with our more boisterous activities. These included 'British Bulldog' a game whose object was to hop with arms folded and attack anybody in sight and knock them off balance. We also played this at Staples Road School and later at Buckhurst Hill County High but I remember being surprised to read that most, if not all, schools have now banned it on health and safety grounds.

Church parade services were conducted by Mr McKelvie, the Union Church minister at the time. They were taken very seriously, as no doubt was the case in other local packs, and we had to have a very good excuse for non-attendance. My final parade was probably in 1954 or 1955 when I left the Scouts, but easily the most memorable were those on Remembrance Sundays of some years earlier when I was still a Cub, as every youth and Services organisation in Loughton turned out in force before marching to stirring music through the crowded town to the War Memorial.

These days most carol singers, normally two or three nervous pre-teens, will tamely sing the first two or three lines of a carol (it always seems to be *Good King Wenceslas*), one verse if you are lucky, before waving a tin under your nose. In fact, many more children seem to turn out, in our road at least, for 'trick or treat' on Halloween, which seems very much in fashion now. It was different for some years in the early 50s when 20 or more from the Union Church, Guides, Scouts and older members of the congregation would perform enthusiastically on two or three separate December days at strategic points in Ollards Grove, Connaught Avenue, Meadow Road and other roads near the church. It was the full works, with comprehensive song sheets, somebody carrying an oil lantern on a pole, and another holding a card showing the name of the organisation that would benefit from our efforts. We always had an excellent response and rarely had to knock on doors, as people would come outside to listen, sometimes even to join in, before giving generously. It may read like a Christmas cliché but when, as happened sometimes, we were singing in the snow we were often offered hot drinks to fend off the cold. I'm sure the Union Church street singers of the 50s weren't the only ones carolling in this way and perhaps similar groups still sing out. For example the Methodist Church still do this every year, collecting around the Habgood Estate for 'NCH – action for Children' and St Mary's still sing carols in Loughton Station.

With encouragement from our teachers, the majority of my Staples Road classmates attended either church or Sunday school, but in my seven years there, 1945–1952, probably more of them went to St Mary's in the middle of town than anywhere else. I remember a number of services held there when Staples Road pupils gave readings, sang solos or formed the choir, particularly those when I was a reader and when we performed our nativity play: on both occasions the church was packed.

For many current Loughton dwellers, however lightly or devoutly they observe their particular faith, there is probably one building with more significance for them than any other. It may be the Loughton Union Church, Loughton Methodist, St Edmund's, St Mary's, St John's, St Michael's, maybe the Forest Hall or perhaps the nearest synagogue or a mosque. No doubt all these have been, and still are, a source of comfort, support and happy memories but, as it is impossible to do justice to them in this short chapter, I will not try.

Like very many neighbours and others from Smarts Lane 50 or 60 years ago, well before that in our family's case, the most influential church was St Mary's. My grandparents were married there in 1910: Mary, my grand-mother died in 1967, her husband, Harry in 1969 and both funerals were held there. My cousin Ron married Pauline at St Mary's in 1955 and when his parents, May and Harry, died their funerals, like my parents' also took place there. With the exception of my mother's, all those funerals were handled by Warriners in Church Hill, the choice of many of our neigh-bours. Dan Warriner is now retired but still, I understand, does the occa-sional funeral for friends. He was always an impressive sight walking ahead of a funeral cortège, maintaining a slow dignified pace past numer-ous bowed heads to the end of the Lane from where the cars drove slowly on to the church.

Most of my relatives, like many others from the road, are buried in Loughton Cemetery in Church Lane, next to St John's. This cemetery dates from the 1880s but when my father died in 1982 we were told there was no room for more grave spaces so he could not be buried near his parents, but was instead interred in the new Chigwell Cemetery in Grange Hill, to be joined by my mother 20 years later.

When Pauline and cousin Ron (who sadly died in June this year) were married, the reception was held in his parents' house, as was sometimes the case among our neighbours in the 50s when money was limited. The small front room of 47 Smarts Lane, probably no more than 14 feet long and a lot less wide, saw the beginning of a marriage that has so far lasted over 50 years. In the 50s and 60s I attended other weddings at St Mary's, some of fellow cricketers, after which the receptions were often held in the Lopping Hall, a favourite for that purpose in those days. Another venue, although much less popular, was Lincoln Hall, opposite the Union Church, and now used by the Red Cross. Pauline and Ron's daughter, Karen, married John in St Mary's, but their reception was held in St Olave's Hotel, that later became the Loughton Park Hotel, now yet another of Loughton's mushrooming apartment blocks. There used to be another hotel nearby, the Wilrae, now a private medical clinic.

In the 50s, although less so in the 60s, courtship and marriage still involved much more formality than now. For example, 50s parents, especially in Loughton, a town which more than most believed in long-held traditions, expected to be asked properly for their daughter's hand in marriage. If couples didn't marry they 'lived in sin', 'partners' were unacceptable and attitudes in the 50s, even into the 60s, were unsympathetic towards unmarried mothers, many of whom had to have their babies adopted. For instance the sign in Station Road proclaiming 'St Faith's Home for Unmarried Mothers' sometimes gave rise to various catty comments. The conventions were strict and it was very rare in the 50s for unescorted girls to visit pubs anywhere in the town, although the more adventurous, including a few from Smarts Lane, would often pair up and go off to dance halls in the West End or nearer ones such as the Ilford Palais and the Walthamstow Assembly Hall.

Many Loughton married couples either met at youth clubs, dances organised by local societies, old boys' associations or at gatherings such as church socials. Early in the period, even though the Second World War led to a dismantling of some old social barriers, the town remained stubbornly stratified compared with many other places and it was slow to change. Most weddings were between couples of similar class or standing. That changed a lot as the 50s progressed and, as well as more weddings of couples from different backgrounds, there were also, as lingering mutual caution between the two communities evaporated, more marriages among residents of the old Loughton and the expanding Debden Estate.

101

Local sport, especially cricket, for example, Old Buckwellians' matches, also led to introductions, then relationships and finally marriage, sometimes through players' sisters first coming along to watch, then joining in the post-match social side. Many couples, Sandra and myself included, met through our work, probably the most frequent way in which serious relationships began, and even though by then the 60s were well advanced I sought her father's consent in the traditional manner.

For many of us, even in a largely affluent town such as Loughton, organising our social activities wasn't always easy. It may seem unimaginable in these days of sophisticated communications and mobile phones but in the 50s telephones were a still a rarity in Smarts Lane and similar less well-off parts. Those with a phone were normally quite happy to allow neighbours to use it, and some even had a box next to it for the cost of the call. However, many preferred to walk into town to a public call box. Whenever I wanted to make a call it meant going to the pair of call boxes on the side of Hutchins the chemist, near the old drinking fountain. (It was in fact a replacement fountain for the one demolished by a bus in the early 30s). Both those telephone boxes were frequently out of order or there might be people already waiting to use them but, fortunately, as I was known in the Loughton Club where I was allowed to play table tennis, I was able, at least until the mid-50s, to use their pay-phone in the booth in the lobby, which was very quiet and cosy, and where nobody knocked impatiently on the window urging you to get a move on.

Quite a number of my friends also had no phone so it was often easier to organise our social lives simply by popping round to each other on our bikes. I frequently argued with my father about having the telephone installed, but he remained adamant that we had no need of one and it wasn't until the late 70s, not long before he died, that he finally relented. For years he had said that other people in Smarts Lane managed quite well without a telephone and that we would be 'living above our station' by having one ourselves when we didn't need it. Perhaps that says quite a lot about some of Loughton's older residents of that time and about an earlier social order they couldn't entirely forget.

20 A stroll down Smarts Lane

In case anything interesting had slipped my memory about what was once the poorest and yet is possibly the most historic street in Loughton, I took the dog for a slow stroll up and down Smarts Lane, my old road. I decided to leave my car somewhere handy in the Lane itself and then take a careful look around but while searching for a free space I became acutely aware of probably the most obvious difference between the road of over half a century ago and now, namely, the near impossibility of finding somewhere to park. From the very top of Smarts Lane, at the junction with Forest Road, right to the bottom and the full car park on the former site of Victor's handyman's shop, there was not a single space left, the result of cars already parked in the road and of residents' dropped kerbs.

There was also no room in High Beech Road, Forest Road or in the Carpenters' Arms, Victoria Tavern and Royal Oak car parks but I was finally lucky in the tiny car park in front of the Stubbles, the forest clearing off Nursery Road.

Smarts Lane was so different at the start of the 50s. Like many of Loughton's streets, it seemed much more relaxed all those years ago than on the hot July afternoon in 2005 that I chose for my quiet walk. Cars were probably more scarce in our road than anywhere in Loughton, and it was still a two-way street (as it would be for almost another 10 years) but it was always easy for Fosters' or other firms' lorries to drive up and down, or for the men on various horse-drawn carts to make their deliveries. A later 1958 photograph of the former British School which was opposite our house, taken by Chris Johnson, also shows the Lane from that point almost to the bottom of the road. In that photo, in which almost half the road is visible, there is one van, one car, a motor-cycle combination and a scooter, otherwise the street is clear and that is how I remember it.

The exit from the Stubbles car park almost faces the 'Green' at the corner of Smarts Lane and Nursery Road and comparing that small clearing with the past the first impression is that it seems much smaller than it did 50 or so years ago, probably because the trees and bushes have now encroached so much. It still looks attractive, especially after the grass has been freshly cut, as had been done that day, but the inside of that small wood was somewhat disheartening. There used to be a clear walkway through those trees, starting at the tiny path opposite the Victoria Tavern, and emerging where Connaught Avenue joins Nursery Road, but when I tried it, although so much of Epping Forest has been greatly improved by the City of London, the first part of this little walk seemed to have been overlooked and badly obstructed by fallen and discarded debris, it needed a good tidy up.

The mix of buildings was different in the 50s and 60s. Between the rows of terraced cottages and pairs of either brick or weather-boarded small dwellings were various business premises, some large, others simply small shops or sheds used for a variety of trades. Now the road is almost entirely residential as nearly all the former businesses are gone, having been replaced by housing developments with even more house building in the pipeline.

Starting at the top of the Lane, the first commercial premises still in existence are rather hidden away beside Upper Belle Vue Cottages and are not much more than garages/sheds. Electrical repairs were carried out on my very first car, a secondhand Ford Anglia, in one of those 43 years ago. I didn't look too closely, but at least some of the sheds still seemed to be in daily use although Chris Pond points out that soon after my stroll, planning permission was given for residential development on this site and the buildings were sold in October, 2005.

Upper Belle Vue Cottages appear to be the only visibly named terrace in the road although at the top of the little alley next door there is an arrow indicating 1–3 Lower Belle Vue Cottages. No 1 was the home of the late Harry Willingale and his son, Tom, now also deceased, descendants of the family which included Thomas Willingale, the main fighter for the loppers' rights, after which the Lopping Hall, funded from their compensation money, is named. Harry was a very friendly man who often sat outside the Carpenters' Arms which he seemed to prefer to other pubs in the Lane and in later years Tom would spend hours leaning on the fence at the top of his alley, watching the world go by.

Most of these small houses have now had their old sash windows replaced with mass produced UPVC double glazing but although that has altered their appearance quite appreciably, as with many others in the road, it is only when I walked down the little alley and looked at the back of the cottages that the true size and scale of some of the more significant alterations became clear. In some cases the extensions relative to the size of the original dwelling, are huge, so that many are now a very far cry from the original little two-up, two-downs I remember. There are a number of those tiny access alleyways between other terraces in Smarts Lane, and when I had a look down them the story was much the same. As well as more double glazing, added-on bay windows or porches, most of those small dwellings have also been greatly increased in volume and the interiors probably bear little resemblance to the small back room, scullery and outside lavatory days I recall so well.

Houses in Smarts Lane of the 50s whether brick or weatherboard were, with a few exceptions small, and some of them particularly so. They were originally low cost homes for working class labourers, shop assistants, railway workers, public servants and those in the service of wealthy families of much earlier days and many of the residents living in them when I was very young were still in similar jobs.

Most of the old cottages in the Lane and in Beech Terrace, an attractive little cluster of nine cottages tucked between Nos 50 and 52, are now freehold and have been extensively modernised, but in the 50s renting was the norm and home improvements were very rare. As well as landlords such as the Chiswells and Goulds, many residents from wealthier roads or local business people also owned one or two cottages or houses in different parts of the town as an investment, usually employing a third party manager/rent collector to protect their interests. Many tenants I remember from Smarts Lane, including my grandparents and Uncle Harry, were content to pay rent all their lives and for all I know some of those still living may have continued to do so. I know that, as one would expect, there are various 'buy to lets' in Smarts Lane but I'm not sure whether there are any situations directly comparable to the two Chris Pond mentioned to me in

Staples Road, with a controlled rent in 2004 of about £90 per week. One of those, with no bathroom, has since been sold for about £230,000.

My grandmother always used to keep the rent tucked inside a little green book and the night before the rent man called she would put it on a small shelf inside the front door. For many years until Nan and Granddad became too frail, that front door was never locked and if the collector knocked but failed to get an answer, he would step inside, take the money and mark off the book by way of receipt. There was never any problem, and the same informal arrangement applied to John Forbes, a well-known figure around the town and for many years a dogged opening batsman with South Loughton Cricket Club. John was the 'man from the Prudential' who made weekly door-to-door collections on his bike, sometimes from residents who had been paying tiny premiums for a long time to make sure they had enough to cover their funeral expenses.

A little further down the Lane I had a good look at the Victoria Tavern which now backs on to the Royal Oak. Both pubs have pleasant beer gardens, although something of the homely character of the Vic has been changed by the loss of the big aviary many customers used to find so satisfying. I was also slightly troubled by the warnings and disclaimers at several points outside the pubs including amongst others, pronouncements such as: 'Dogs must be on a lead at all times . . . Strictly no bicycles allowed in the garden . . . Children must be supervised at all times . . . We accept no liability for injury or damage whilst on these premises . . . No public right of way exists.'

No doubt it's all a sign of the times but it reminds you that 50 or so years ago some aspects of life in places like Loughton were more free and easy than now. Those who went to pubs in Smarts Lane then weren't threatened with being clamped or fined £80 and, for their part, landlords of those times probably had no worries about being sued.

As for businesses from the 50s and 60s that are gone, the first one I remembered on this stroll was the little antique shop opposite the Victoria Tavern, on the fork of Smarts Lane and High Beech Road. Now a house, it was formerly Locks, a sweetshop-cum-grocers and before that a tea-room catering for day trippers to the Forest. A bit further down on the opposite side at 113 Smarts Lane is a new row of houses on the site of what was known as Cole's yard. J Cole and Sons was one of the Lane's largest businesses, operating as a haulage and car hire company, founded by Jack Cole, (christened John) joined later by his four sons and Ida, his daughter. The brothers also ran smallholdings in Coles Green, a turning off Goldings Road, and also down Stony Path, off Baldwins Hill. At first Jack used horse-drawn carts but later lorries as well, and Cole's were active participants in the town's carnivals and other celebrations. Many floats had their final touches added in that yard. Other traders, including the coalman, Tom Willingale, stabled horses there, and for some years the premises next door were used as a depot by Walls, the ice cream manufacturers.

Almost opposite at No 86 was Askew's yard (one of two they owned, the other being in Buckhurst Hill), where the family straw and hay distribution business was conducted, yet another that closed many years ago. Their horse-drawn carts and later their lorries, piled unbelievably high with bales, used to operate both locally and well into Essex and East Anglia.

By far the largest business in Smarts Lane, and for many years the most well-known of all Loughton's building firms was Charles S Foster & Sons Ltd which together with its associated company, Essex Steel Scaffolding, occupied an extensive complex of buildings and yards stretching 80 yards or more up the west side of the Lane from No 14, next to Forest House, formerly Frank Button's little sweet shop. The yard then continued in a curve quite a way behind some of the existing weather-boarded houses. Charles Savin Foster was living in High Beech Road when he founded the firm and one of his sons, Frank, later Sir Frank, as well as being involved in the firm, became chairman of the local council and then of the Essex County Council. Fosters' motto was 'A builder's work is his best advertisement' and for many years my grandfather worked for them and Uncle Harry for Essex Steel. As I never heard them complain about their jobs I assume they were happy with their employers. Foster's ceased trading when the firm could no longer exist purely as a family business. The rather stark main building with its great loading bay was bought by Magnet Joinery and was one of their outlets for a while, although I don't believe it was ever a very profitable one. Fosters' old arc-shaped yard is now a private car park while all the buildings fronting Smarts Lane were demolished to make way for modern terraced and semi-detached houses.

One of those houses was occupied by a bowls friend, the late Chris English, who had been a very senior manager with one of the major banks. Some years after being widowed he decided to downsize from his large house and grounds in Spareleaze Hill into one of the new properties and probably as much as anything else that seems to illustrate how Loughton's perception of Smarts Lane has changed over the last 50 years.

Our old house, No 73, is now a spacious, even slightly up-market property, although the parking arrangements leave something to be desired. Gertrude Green, of *My Life in Loughton* fame, who lived at No 69, would certainly be unable to recognise her old house, nor the old British School opposite, Nos 42–44, which has been transformed into quite a substantial four-bedroomed property. No 47, where Uncle Harry's family lived, was also enlarged and brought completely up-to-date, with a bathroom upstairs, not as some others were, simply stuck on the back, and for some time in the 90s it was rented to a successful young City friend of my elder son.

Building is still going on down those little alleys and narrow drives, in some cases transforming semi-derelict old sites into modern dwellings. For example, at the time of writing, my old garage, never really much more than a glorified shed tucked away behind small cottages near the bottom of the road, and which I rented for 12s. 6d. a week in 1962, seems to have been cleared to make way for yet another new development.

Many houses in the road have had their front gardens converted to hard-standing for cars but some scarcely have room for much more than a Mini to park without overhanging the pavement. That was almost unheard of 50 years ago when the road was virtually bare of cars and at lunchtime my father would often return home in Eaton's lorry which he would simply leave outside the house without ever blocking anybody's way.

He would sometimes come home on his old bike, perhaps having called at his allotment in Roding Road, where a few other men from the lane also rented plots. It was not unusual to see him pushing the bike up the road with a sack of potatoes or other vegetables on the handlebars or stuffed into bags over the crossbar. Mr Brewster from No 78 had a plot very close to ours and the allotments were an important part of both their lives. Rain or shine both he and my father would spend many hours each week down there. It was a trusting little community and most of the holders had small sheds or large storage boxes for tools which were rarely locked so that they could freely borrow each other's equipment. There were never any problems until, for the first time that my father could remember, probably in 1953–54 tools, seed or fertiliser started to go missing. After that Dad would always lock up, which he said was a shame but at least from then right until the late 70s when he gave the plot up he had no more trouble. I believe the annual fee for the plots when he started there in the late 40s was about 7s. 6d. probably rising to few pounds by the time he finished. It seems those plots can now be rented at £19 a year.

Besides Frank Button's shop, now housing an avant-garde children's education centre, other small premises that have been altered or have disappeared altogether include Grimsleys the butcher, Street's Dairy, the Loughton Poultry and Rabbit Club and the later Brown's garden machinery business right at the end of the road. Some readers may recall and miss some of these and think it is a pity that Smarts Lane is not as rural or as pleasant as it once was. Although there is probably some truth in that, there is also no doubt that if they were still alive many of the Lane's former residents would be pleased to know that it is no longer looked upon as the very humblest of Loughton's streets.

On the way back to the car I called in at the Carpenters' Arms which by then was very quiet. It is still nicely old-fashioned inside and on the wall there are some excellent old photos of Loughton. Best of all, much as it would have been 50 or more years ago and very welcome on such a hot day, a bowl of water for thirsty dogs stood in the old fireplace.

21 And finally . . .

Although the centre part of our cluttered High Road, with its uncoordinated shop fronts and the same financial and retail group branches as those cloned in hundreds of other places, may not be Loughton's most attractive feature nor appeal as much as the more harmonious and tranquil thoroughfare of only 50 years earlier, the town's many other charms cannot be ignored. The Epping Forest location, green views and nature reserves combine with a host of listed buildings and quaint cottages in little alleys and quiet by-ways to prevent Loughton from becoming simply another run-of-the-mill suburban dormitory town. It would be easy to grouse like a latter-day Victor Meldrew but, although many older Loughtonians may feel nostalgic about the town, or 'the village' as it was still known in the 50s and 60s, those from succeeding generations seem mainly happy with the way it is today so it is unproductive to indicate an overall preference. Some of the changes have been mentioned in other chapters but a few concluding reflections come to mind.

Although many residents found day-to-day living a struggle Loughton recovered quicker than most places from post-war austerity and remained an affluent town throughout the 50s, 60s and beyond. Perhaps one difference between then and now is that 60 years ago the wealthiest Loughtonians were generally those with family capital or from the professional classes who were also used to having money but who, for the most part, were disinclined to draw attention to it. It is still a wealthy town, as can be seen from the expensive boutiques, home improvement shops, estate agents, financial services outlets and up-market eating places that now fill the High Road, as well as from the high price of property and the ongoing residential development here. The town's location with such easy access to London and the massive, albeit under-used, bonus of the Forest, has sent prices rocketing and from time to time Loughton with its scores of £1 million plus houses has been cited as one of Britain's 'property hotspots'. Now the town's wealthier individuals come from many diverse backgrounds and for some at least all former inhibitions about displaying their affluence seem to have been completely dispelled.

Loughton's social order changed a lot after the Second World War, but it took a long time for some of the barriers to fall, probably longer here than in most places, as the town remained one that clung quite stubbornly to its traditional ways. I knew a number of Loughtonians who had been employed as domestic servants by the town's wealthy families and whose relatives before them had earned their living in the same way. For example, in her younger days my grandmother was in service for a time as a resident housemaid in Church Hill, one of quite a number in Smarts Lane and Forest Road formerly dependent on such employment. After the Second World War many Loughtonians from the next generation, such as my mother, supplemented their budgets by cleaning wealthier families' houses. Although demand for domestic help was high the days of full-time service had gone and as a consequence many of the town's older and larger properties became increasingly difficult to maintain, so becoming an easy target for redevelopment.

These days many wealthy young Loughton couples, especially if both are working, pay for gardeners, home helps, car cleaners, crèches and nurseries, and many businesses, from sole traders upwards, have sprouted to meet this demand. There is a need, and many enterprising people, some in their 20s and 30s, are charging a high price to fill it. However, at least among the many Loughtonians I know who use these services, there is no question of class difference, least of all the pre-war master and servant pattern.

Another obvious change over the last 60 years is in the town's traffic. I don't think it is too controversial to say that although cars have improved immensely, local driving hasn't. Not only are there vastly more cars in Loughton now, but some seem to be driven in a different way, and quite a few motorists in the town have – as elsewhere – become extremely aggressive.

After the Second World War many cars came out of their garages for the first time in five years or so, and it wasn't until the 60s that car ownership, even in a wealthy town like ours, really took off. Many roads seemed almost empty and you could park for free virtually anywhere. Mothers with pushchairs didn't have to walk in the road to avoid cars parked on the pavement, one-way streets were rare, speed humps didn't exist and there were no problems with the school run, inconsiderately parked FWDs, or upwardly raised fingers from surprisingly angelic-looking Loughton drivers. One-handed driving and ignoring the laws about mobile phones are now a dangerous but commonplace fact of Loughton life, more so I fancy than in many other places. Another menace are the lazy drivers who deliberately swerve, often with no signal, the wrong way round the various mini-roundabouts along the High Road and elsewhere in and near the town.

However, until the breathalyser, MOT tests and the voluntary use of seat belts were introduced in the 60s (seat belts became obligatory in 1983) there were other risks, and not everything way back was ideal. For example in 1962, for want of a safer car, one of my closest Buckhurst Hill County High friends, David Wilkins, a superb Loughtonian sportsman, lost his life in Broadmead Road, Woodford Green. He was a front seat passenger in a car that, having swerved to avoid a recklessly driven scooter, hit a telegraph pole.

How well did Loughtonians care for the elderly compared to now? I'm sure there is no difference in the will to look after ageing relatives as diligently as possible but there is no doubt it has been made harder locally to provide the care they deserve. All I can say on this topic is that when Mary, my grandmother, died in 1967, her condition was distressing but she stayed in 45 Smarts Lane until the end, nursed, fed, cleaned and cared for by her relatives, attended daily by the doctor, and nothing was too much trouble.

All her adult life Nan had worn her hair in a bun, and that was the only way I had ever seen it, so it was very strange after she died to see her with her hair combed straight, and reaching down to her waist. It was a great shame that a day or so after her death and while my grandfather Harry was still upset, a so-called antique dealer swindled him when he was alone in the house, paying him 30s. for a much prized blue dish, probably Wedgwood or Spode, that stood for many years in the front room window. In those days it was possibly worth more than ten times as much, but the man convinced him that it would help pay for Mary's funeral. His sons Harry and Dick looked high and low for the swindler, but with no luck.

Granddad died peacefully in 1969 in a nursing home in Chigwell, one which the family selected from various excellent local homes offered to us and which was arranged with a minimum of fuss. It was so different when my mother died in 2001. Essex County Council were closing or selling residential homes everywhere and we were told she would have to go to Harlow or Colchester but she refused. She was fortunate to spend a few months in Beechlands in Alderton Hill (the former home of Bernard Gould, of the prominent Loughton family), one of the few remaining ECC care homes, before finally being transferred to Whipps Cross. The financial assessment questionnaire which I had to complete, including all ancillary notes, ran to over 70 pages, and the whole process was dogged by bureaucracy.

Very few of my relatives had any pension apart from that paid by the state, although most of them had at least one small life or endowment policy, often intended to meet funeral expenses. My grandfather and many of his contemporaries in Smarts Lane depended on the state and the 'old age pension'. A generation later, when my father retired from Eaton Bros after working there for over half his life somebody, probably Michael Shingleton, then the firm's general manager, made a short farewell speech. Dad was given a wristwatch, which I still have in its box, paid for by a collection from his workmates. He received nothing else. Fortunately he had saved wisely so when he died my mother was left reasonably placed, but many others I had known from childhood were much less fortunate, although most of them seemed to struggle along somehow. It is ironic that for many from current and future generations inadequate pension provision will be one of the worst problems they will face, and they could well end up in much greater financial difficulty than those who retired in the 50s and 60s.

In those days there seemed to be more linkage than now between those who depended on social services or the Council and those who provided it. Residents of Smarts Lane and Forest Road, and no doubt elsewhere, who worked for the Council half a century ago were proud of that, and their achievements, particularly in the winters of 1947 and 1962–63 were widely praised. Nowadays there seems to be a remoteness about our local service providers. Problems get passed from person to person, there is limited meaningful discussion about important issues and so we are often presented with a *fait accompli*. There often seems to be much less determination to press on in the face of even the slightest difficulty, as evidenced by the chaos caused by the few inches of snow that fell on Loughton in the 2004–5 winter. However, it seems fair to say that at the time of writing in mid-January, the winter of 2005–6 has caused relatively few problems.

Nowadays, as elsewhere, Loughtonians watch their children or grandchildren every minute they are outside the house even, as in our road, if they are only walking 50 yards or so to the nearby pillar box. Few primary school pupils walk to school now and parents, aware of tragedies involving children in other parts, are rightfully concerned to protect their own. Current Loughtonians might think there were no problems 50 or 60 years ago as we often spent hours, or sometimes a whole day, playing in the street or in Epping Forest, or, aged from five or six, we would walk on our own to Staples Road School. That was largely true, despite the fact that the Forest occasionally disclosed a darker side and, as happens now, various unpleasant individuals would lurk inside.

One of the worst local incidents on record, but nothing to do with the Forest, took place in Loughton in the late 50s, a dreadful episode which at the time changed attitudes about allowing Loughton's children as much freedom as they had been used to.

Allan Warren, 7, of Carlton Colville, Suffolk, was on holiday with his family, staying with his uncle, Colin Warren, of Smarts Lane. He was abducted from a car outside the Crown in Loughton High Road on Saturday, 10 August 1957, and his body was found on the site of a new house in Connaught Hill on the 11th. He had been sexually assaulted, stripped naked and asphyxiated. His clothes were found on the Central Line at Bethnal Green.

Horace Henry Edwards, 36, a bench hand from Wanstead, was charged with his murder. He had tried to commit suicide. There were demonstrations when he appeared at Epping Court and later relatives, friends and others organised local petitions seeking maximum justice. He eventually pleaded guilty and was sentenced to life imprisonment at the Old Bailey on 26 October 1957.

Although relatively few current Loughton residents may be aware of that case, I am certain those who do know about it find it hard to condemn current parents who might seem excessively zealous in protecting their children. We may feel uneasy at the way 'yob culture' affects such a mainly privileged community as Loughton, and about the need to impose ASBOs, with hosts of youngsters, especially at weekends, milling around the station or throughout the town. Some of them are probably carrying some sort of weapon, but the event just described puts even that into a wider perspective. Ironically, although unprovoked assaults in the town in the 50s and 60s were uncommon, Loughton Station was probably the area where most care was needed, particularly in the foul-smelling graffiti-covered subway leading to the pathway alongside the old Roding Road school fields. A number of disturbing incidents, mostly involving female residents, took place there.

Fifty years ago Loughtonians could choose from various local newspapers. We had the *West Essex Gazette* and the *Express and Independent,* plus others that concentrated on Chigwell and Woodford. Through closures, mergers and changes of name we now have only the one, the Loughton, Buckhurst Hill, Chigwell and now Waltham Abbey edition of the *Guardian,* which covers a much wider area of West Essex. It seems a pity that as a consequence the Loughton focus is now lost in a welter of items about other towns. We always buy it each week, but sometimes miss some of the quaintness of the journals of those earlier times, reporting such trivia as some wicked Loughtonian being fined 10s. for having no rear light on his bike, or perhaps £1 for being drunk and disorderly outside the Carpenters' Arms or the Victoria Tavern. The letters, which were often the best part of the paper, were more interesting, too; these days most are deadly dull as so many tit-for-tat political punches are traded every week in the *Guardian's* columns. Fair enough when elections are being contested, but most of the many people I know who buy the paper look first at the names at the end of each letter, and the ones that seem likely to be yet another out-of-season party political are left unread.

One event well covered in the local press in 1967 was the visit of the Dutch hockey club, Push Breda, to play against the Farmers, the festival side made up mainly of Old Buckwellians and Old Loughtonians. This was a wonderful annual event that continued for some years, alternating between Holland and England, with players staying in each other's homes, and some of the friendships made in those days still continue. Having been kept going by sheer will-power and sticking plaster, the Farmers still manage to turn out a side each Easter. I have a group photograph of the 1967 teams and guests, taken in front of Loughton's old Council offices. Prominent in that is Tony Swallow, wearing his chain of office as Chairman of the Chigwell UDC, and also George Shuttlewood. Many will remember George (who lived in Grange Court in the High Road) with immense affection. For many years he was a regular Old Buckwellian and Farmers' hockey umpire but is perhaps much better remembered as one of Loughton Cricket Club's leading officials, standing for many years in his spotless white coat. George was the fairest adjudicator I ever met even admitting, for bowlers, his reluctance ever to uphold an LBW appeal, which to my fellow players and myself naturally seemed plumb, sometimes made us frustrated. However, it all balanced out nicely as our batsmen knew that if we got hit on the pads 99% of any appeals, no matter how frenzied, would be turned down.

Local club cricket in the 40s and 50s was avidly followed by many town residents, and the oldest rivalry was between Loughton and Buckhurst Hill. 'The Hill' as we called them, were the district's top dogs in those days, although that is no longer the case. I played in a number of memorable matches but even in the 60s, when the Essex League started, there was nothing to compare with the contests between the two sides that I watched as a youth in the early 50s. These twice-a-season matches were normally on Bank Holidays, and for a time enthusiasm was so great that scorecards would be printed and sold for 3d. Hundreds would watch and even bring beer and sandwiches, crowding the benches on the High Road boundary or on the grass under the magnificent row of elms that used to flank the Traps Hill side. Many who were there must remember such performers as Pat Shott (possibly the best club cricketer I ever saw), Nick Madgwick, Lance Carter, Rex Roberts and Gordon Spooner, to name but a few.

By sheer coincidence, as I was working on this final chapter I met Rodney Barratt, another old Smarts Lane resident. Rodney, who came from probably the largest family in Smarts Lane, is one of 10 children. It would have been 12, but there were twins who sadly did not survive. He is one year older than me and also attended Staples Road School. Now a local builder, he is a member of the Loughton and District Historical Society, but it was in his professional capacity that we were reunited after a gap of about 47 years. As well as reminiscing about many of the events already described he revived a few extra memories of our early days in Loughton for which I am grateful.

Frank Button, the little short-sighted man who ran the sweet shop at the bottom of Smarts Lane, would often go into the back of his shop to sort out an order. In the late 40s the shop was still gas-lit and while Frank was in the back some of the lads from the road would reach up and turn the gas down a bit. The resulting gloom made it hard for Frank to see what was going on in the front of the shop, so it was much easier to snaffle a few sweets. Eventually Frank twigged who the culprits were and told their parents, who then dealt out instant justice as in those days a clip round the ear, or even something rather more severe was never questioned.

During the years I was allowed to play table-tennis in the Loughton Club my father sometimes talked about the secretive heavy gambling reputed to have taken place there in the years following the Second World War. This was another subject Rodney and I touched on and we both knew some of the men in the Lane who reported very weighty betting there, even to the extent that some Loughton landlords won or lost properties on the turn of a single card. Probably nobody can be sure whether it was true or not, but if it did happen I'm sure the Committee must have been unaware of it. My father, who deplored any form of betting, also knew of serious gambling in the Forest, and that Fairmead Bottom, off Nursery Road, was a venue for some very high-stake games.

Tom Willingale, Harry's son, mentioned earlier, was a coalman for years and kept his horse in Ida Cole's yard, about 60 yards past the Carpenters Arms on the way to the Forest (not to be confused with the unrelated *Ada* Cole of local stables fame). Tom would take the horse and cart down to the coal yards near Loughton Station and load up, stabling the horse when his round was finished. Something I heard about but didn't see myself was that one evening the horse ran amok up and down Smarts Lane. For some reason, maybe being attacked by a horsefly, a nasty blood-sucker which can give a really vicious bite, or simply frustrated at being confined, it went berserk and kicked its way out of its stall before, foaming at the mouth, shooting off towards Epping Forest. After much trouble and a united rescue operation it was restored to the stables. Tom Willingale passed away in 2003.

I have already mentioned Jack Street, the well-known Smarts Lane dairyman, but he was not the only man delivering milk. Ruddock from near the Owl at High Beach was another milkman who delivered in Loughton, but for some reason Jack seemed more popular and his horses, particularly Robin, his last one, were more docile. One day some lads from Smarts Lane and Forest Road were in the Forest opposite Staples Road, near the Staples Hill Path which connects Staples Road to The Drive. Ruddock was delivering milk from his horse-drawn cart, which was tied to a lamppost. The boys, armed with long home-made pea shooters, opened fire on his horse and the wretched animal, apparently unstable even at the best of times, bucked and kicked as the pellets connected with its flank. The front of the cart was smashed, it tipped, bottles, churns and jugs tumbled onto the road, only to be sent flying even further as the demented horse lashed out with its back legs. I don't know the aftermath, and even if I could guess who fired the pellets I'm not saying.

Rodney also reminded me of a bad case of bullying that was summarily sorted out. A Smarts Lane resident, who I remember but will not name, but who was notably tall, probably six feet four or five and very powerful, hit a young member of a family in the Lane very hard. The lad's elder brother, quite big himself, but well short of the bully, chased him up Smarts Lane wielding a broom handle, which he broke in half over his head, thereby meting out instant justice. This spectacular retribution wasn't reported to the police, there was no need, it was over. Despite some of the earlier hardships, we normally got on well with each other in the Lane but occasionally frustrations boiled over, and I did see other occasional in-stances of reprisal and retaliation, although not as dramatic as this one.

I have previously described the generosity of Mr and Mrs Howes, the greengrocers, in providing fireworks for the late 40s/early 50s Guy Fawkes' night displays on the green at the top of Smarts Lane, but Rodney remem-bers that their kindness went even further. In those days not everybody in the Lane could afford fruit and it was often scarce anyway. The Howes' would bring crates of fruit, mainly oranges, to the display and make sure everybody, especially the children, had a fair share, so adding to the pleasure of those evenings.

Rodney also reminded me of a little Smarts Lane oddity concerning the fact that, when speaking about where we were going, the word *to* was hardly ever used. We would say we were going *round* the village, *down* the station, *up* the Forest, *on* the Stubbles, or *along* the High Road. Is it still the same? As far as residents of my age and older are concerned, I'm sure it is.

Earlier I mentioned my grandfather calling the Reservoir in Staples Road the 'Reservoy'. I remember my father called the last he used for shoe mending his 'hobbing foot' – it isn't in any of our dictionaries at home, but I traced it on the internet, and he was correct. What is more, I also recall another of my grandfather's mispronunciations, in referring to his own last as his 'hobby foot'.

Other words and turns of phrase used by older residents from Smarts Lane and elsewhere certainly seemed to have their own special flavour. Examples include: 'dods' or 'doddies' – snails; 'donkeys years' – a long time ago; 'learn' for teach, as in 'that'll learn yer'; 'pay' – to hit, e.g. 'I'll pay you for that'; 'threadle' – to thread, always used by my grandmother, as was the frequent use of 'do' by my grandfather, as in 'she do hate house-work', 'he do love that dog'. A different 'do', common in Smarts Lane and the poorer roads, meant to clean wealthier people's houses. Yet another was 'I'll do for you' – I'll hurt you.

Wallers Hoppet, a fairly new turning off Woodbury Hill, owes its name to the old Essex word for a small meadow close to habitation where sick animals could recuperate. No doubt some readers can add other words to this list, if they can 'mind' – i.e. remember – them.

This leads to the wider question of a Loughton accent. From my generation onwards, the proximity of London, particularly the East End, has probably exerted more influence on the way we speak in Loughton than any closeness to East Anglia. For example, partly in the period covered by this book, substantial population migration from London into Essex, including to new towns and estates may have given a considerable boost to what now seems to be called Estuary English, even 'Mockney'. Now though, the Loughton accent seems much the same as in many other places in the Southeast, particularly as far as younger people are concerned. Any remaining influence on accent associated with the East End may itself be undergoing change as that area becomes more multiracial.

I am grateful for the fact that a combination of the facilities in and around the town plus inherited local traits of stubbornness, perseverance, perhaps the 'street wisdom' of the residents from the poorer roads, provided a solid platform for life.

Loughton's post-war adherence to some elements of an older social order may have irritated some residents, but for the most part any former stratification has long since disappeared and most of us seem content and at ease with it. Many of the changes described in these pages are similar to those in countless other communities and it remains an excellent place to live. Loughton may have had to move with the times but the determination of many concerned local people to preserve as much as possible of what is so good about their town will no doubt guarantee its continued attraction.

I obviously knew that some of my Loughton contemporaries had already died, but after listening to Rodney's recollections I realised the list, including some who departed in middle age or before, is even longer than I thought. I will not mention any names but I wish to pay respect to those who have passed on, as well as to thank those who are still with us, for their contribution to these memories of our town.

Chris Pond suggested that some readers might be interested to know what happened after I left Buckhurst Hill County High School. I studied accountancy and economics at City of London College and entered the City with an institutional stockbrokers. After joining a larger firm I became a member of the London Stock Exchange. In 1986, following 'Big Bang', we were acquired by Barclays Bank. After specialising in local authority pension funds for many years I concentrated exclusively on investment in Japan. From 1992 to 1996 I was in charge of Barclays' investment management company in Tokyo, and also President of the group's Trust Bank there. Although retired from the bank, I still maintain contact with Tokyo through consultancy work. Sandra and I were married in 1965; we have two sons, each of whom has a son and a daughter.